MW01088715

ASTROLOGY
I^{FOR}NITIATES

The French physician, Papus (Gerard Encausse, 1865–1916) was involved in many secret societies, and was in a unique position to synthesize these influences into his astrological and esoteric work. His mentors included Francois Charles Berlet, the French astrologer involved in the Hermetic Brotherhood of Luxor, and Thomas Burgoyne, author of *The Light of Egypt*, the book that explained the practices of the Hermetic Brotherhood. *Initiation Astrologique* was published in France posthumously in 1920, and made available material used by European esotericists early in the 20th century.

ASTROLOGY
FOR
INITIATES

Astrological Secrets of the
Western Mystery Tradition

PAPUS

Translated with an introduction by
J. Lee Lehman, Ph.D.

SAMUEL WEISER, INC.

York Beach, Maine

First published in 1996 by
Samuel Weiser, Inc.
P. O. Box 612
York Beach, ME 03910-0612

Library of Congress Cataloging-in-Publication Data

Papus, 1865–1916.
    [Initiation astrologique.   English]
    Astrology for initiates : astrological secrets of the western
mystery tradition / Papus ; translated by J. Lee Lehman.
        p.   cm.
    Originally published: Paris : vend Se à La Sirène, 1920?
    Includes bibliographical references (p. 127) and index.
    ISBN 0–87728–894–1 (pbk. : alk. paper)
    1. Astrology.   I. Title.
BF1701.P1713   1996
133.5—dc20   96–28287
                                                                   CIP

BJ

Typeset in 11 point Palatino

Printed in the United States of America

04   03   02   01   00   99   98   97   96
10   9   8   7   6   5   4   3   2   1

The paper used in this publication meets the minimum requirements of
the American National Standard for Permanence of Paper for Printed
Library Materials Z39.48–1984.

TABLE OF CONTENTS

TRANSLATOR'S INTRODUCTION

*A beginning is the time for taking the most delicate
care that balances are correct.*
                                    —Frank Herbert, *Dune*

THE FRENCH PHYSICIAN PAPUS (Gérard Encausse,
1865–1916) is best known to English-speaking readers for his
work, *The Tarot of the Bohemians.*[1] However, his influence in late
19th-early 20th-century France was much greater. To understand his position, and the significance of this work, we must
weave together several themes: occultism in the late 19th century and astrology in the same period. Several significant trib-
utaries join the river that was occultism then, and several
emerge into the delta of the late 20th-century New Age.

If v·e begin our examination a bit before the time of
Papus, we can note that the end of the 18th century marked
a considerable uptick of interest in occultism corresponding
to the archaeological successes in Italy, the Middle East, and
Egypt, led primarily by British, German and French teams.
Finally, through the Rosetta stone, Egyptian hieroglyphs became comprehensible to the West. In Italy, Roman life in all
its pagan glory was being unearthed at Pompeii and Hercu-
laneum. The sites of Troy and many biblical locales emerged.
The Western mind confronted the Paganism so thoroughly
repressed by Christianity, just as British and Dutch explorers
and traders in the East were making Buddhist, Hindu, and
Taoist material available in the West on a massive scale. Following the breakdown in the hegemony of the Catholic
Church, for the first time in 1,500 years, it became possible

---

[1] *The Tarot of the Bohemians*, translated by A. P. Morton, with a preface by A. E.
Waite (New York: Samuel Weiser, 1970).

for a Westerner to throw off the yoke of Christianity *without also rejecting spirituality*. This was truly a heady time, one called the Enlightenment.[2]

Elsewhere I have detailed how this influx of knowledge and ideas spawned two New Ages: what I called the Enlightenment New Age in the 18th century, and then, in 1848, the Spiritualist New Age.[3] Briefly, the Spiritualist New Age, which began in the great year of revolutions historically, brought home the immediate idea that death was but a curtain that could, under certain circumstances, be penetrated, at least for purposes of communication.

This pair of New Ages extended across national boundaries in ways that are only now being reestablished. For one thing, the European bias toward multilingual education was still pronounced; for another, many leading practitioners roamed freely between the various European countries, even including America or Asia in their itineraries. Spiritualism itself had begun in the United States, migrating quickly to Europe through such practitioners as Mrs. Hayden and D. D. Home. Enthusiasts in different countries insured that significant works in any language were rapidly translated and transmitted to students of any other language.

Meanwhile, France had its indigenous Spiritualism through the work of Alphonse Cahagnet on his "celestial telegraph." Spiritualism had definite forerunners internationally in mesmerism and crystal scrying, but it only became wildly popular through the coming of the seance.

Later in the century, during the 1870s, interest shifted from communicating with the dead, to the meaning of life in the here-and-now, and also the hereafter. Three major streams

---

[2] The development of occult practices during this period is discussed in detail in Godwin, *The Theosophical Enlightenment* (Albany: State University Press of New York, 1994).

[3] See Lehman, *Classical Astrology for Modern Living* (Atglen, PA: Whitford Press, 1996).

developed in England: the Theosophical Society (T. S.), which was dedicated to the development of a theory of occultism through its exploration of the discoveries and revelations of H. P. Blavatsky *et al.*, revelations that included a substantial portion of Eastern mysticism; the Golden Dawn and related groups, which emphasized the practice of ceremonial magic; and the Hermetic Brotherhood of Luxor (H. B. of L.), a small and curious group that maintained itself along strict Western lines, rejecting such doctrines as reincarnation.[4] Besides these three groups, myriad people and groups styled themselves as Masonic orders, Rosicrucians, or other ancient titles. It was common for individual seekers to accumulate a long pedigree of ranks and memberships in secret, or not-so-secret societies.

During this period, the fate of astrology had differed on the Continent, in England and America. It is overwhelmingly tempting to label the 17th century as the end of the several millennial period of Classical Astrology. The 17th century featured some of the greatest minds of the field: William Lilly, Nicholas Culpeper, Richard Saunders, Placido de Titus and Jean Morin (Morinus), not to mention a second tier that, in almost any other century would be considered the lights: John Gadbury, Richard Edlin, William Ramesey, John Goad and Henry Coley, to name a few.

The 17th century marked the final integration of the idea of the heliocentric solar system, and the victory of scientific materialism as the predominant meta-view of the day. Astrology's fortunes declined markedly in England and the United States in the 18th century, although there is evidence that horary and electional astrology remained popular in port cities

---

[4] Recently many of the primary documents of this organization have become available through the publication by Godwin, Chanel, Deveney, *The Hermetic Brotherhood of Luxor* (York Beach, ME: Samuel Weiser, 1995). This work also documents the troubled relationship of the Hermetic Brotherhood and the Theosophical Society.

for disposition of ships at sea.[5] While astrology didn't disappear from English-speaking countries, those practitioners "remaining" were mostly ignored in the subsequent "revival" in the early 19th century.[6] This subsequent revival, begun popularly by Raphael I and the Mercuri, was of an astrology vastly simplified, often lacking the power to predict. By making a virtue of necessity, British astrology passed from being unable to predict very well to being unwilling to predict at all, in the acceptance of psychological astrology, with its taboos that proscribe activity (such as prediction) that might be seen as impinging on the exercise of free will.

The Continent did not see such extremes in "astrological crash and burn" in the 18th century, and so Continental astrology saw fewer radical changes in fortune in the 19th century.

Knowledge of astrology had long been considered essential to occult learning, being the basis of timing and attribution in alchemy and ritual magic. Its importance to 19th-century occultists increased considerably as archaeological evidence accumulated, which suggested a worldwide primitive state of "star worship," or astrolatry. During this period, one could easily assert the belief that astrolatry was the first major world religion.[7] Thus, astrology became not merely the timepiece of ritual, but the basis for understanding many religious ideas.

---

[5] Robert Zoller has researched this for New York. Evidently both the electional form of picking a time to sail, and the horary form of inquiring after vessels that were overdue were common. Zoller, along with Martin Hausman, have also been able to show that astrological medicine was commonly practiced in immigrant Lutheran communities until at least well into the 19th century.

[6] An extensive discussion of this period can be found in Curry, *A Confusion of Prophets: Victorian and Edwardian Astrology* (London: Collins & Brown, 1992). As he points out, some of the practitioners of the period, such as John Worsdale, were astrological purists, while others, such as the painter John Varley, had broader occult and philosophical interests.

[7] See, for example, works like Mackey, *Mythological Astronomy of the Ancients Demonstrated* (Minneapolis: Wizard's Bookshelf, 1973), which, despite its unfortunate poetry, continued to influence occultists through the rest of the 19th century.

When Papus burst onto the occult scene in 1887, the Theosophical Society was in full swing (it had been founded in 1875), and Thomas Burgoyne's *The Light of Egypt*, a thorough statement of the principles of practices of the H. B. of L., was about to be published in 1889.[8] In 1886, members of the T. S. had discovered that Burgoyne had been convicted of fraud. This discovery virtually destroyed the H. B. of L. in England, although not in France. The reason that the H. B. of L. survived in France is that nearly all the top occultists had ties to it. In the United States, thanks to a generous gift, the H. B. of L. became a parent of the Astro-Philosophical Publishing Company of Denver and the Church of Light, which survives to this day.[9]

The principal of the H. B. of L. in France was François Charles Barlet, who also just happened to be *the* premier French astrologer, and one of Papus' astrological mentors. Papus rapidly became involved in most French occult societies, secret and otherwise. One of his most important contributions was as the publisher of the review *L'initiation*, which was an outlet for such other writers as Eliphas Lévi, Ely Star, and C. Flammarion.

Thus, Papus was situated at the crossroads between many different occult highways. Not having much to do with the T. S., he stayed on the side of more traditional Western occultism, at arm's length from the encroaching influx of Eastern thought through the Theosophical Society.

Papus was part of a global occult community whose enthusiasm for occult material resulted in virtually immediate translation of any important work. While their occult interests were international, curiously their astrology was not: a point that was apparently completely lost on the astrologers of the time. Continental astrologers had stuck more to traditional methods, whereas English astrologers

---

[8] The French language edition was published in 1895. It was later published by the Religio-Philosophical Publishing House in San Francisco (1889).

[9] See Godwin *et al.*, *The Hermetic Brotherhood of Luxor*, pp. 38–39.

had become more intrigued by the newly discovered planets Herschel (Uranus) and Neptune, the asteroids, and later, the hypothetical planets. There was a much stronger seduction of astrology by psychology in English-speaking countries, while on the Continent, especially in French-speaking areas, there was increasing emphasis on so-called scientific method.

Among the curious juxtapositions we encounter through Papus is his use of Thomas Burgoyne as a principal source for astrological methods. Burgoyne's astrology permeated his occultism: for example, Burgoyne followed Mackey's work on pole shifts,[10] correlating historical periods with astrological influences, and giving angels (a very prominent part of the H. B. of L. pantheon) rulership of the planetary energies.[11] Not only did the two-volume *Light of Egypt* contain sixteen (out of forty) chapters specifically on astrology, other chapters contained astrological material as well. Further, these chapters did not merely cover astrology as we might see it in any general astrology text, but also topics such as "astro-theology" and "astro-mythology."

Burgoyne's presentations of the planets, signs, and houses—the three major building blocks of astrology—were

---

[10] The H. B. of L. adopted Mackey as a member: since the H. B. of L. was supposed to extend back to hermetic Egypt, that meant that they could "adopt" any earlier occultist as part of their tradition. Mackey's book covers precession, and the astrological ages of Man [sic], based roughly on the sidereal astrological sign of the Spring Equinox. However, Mackey also presumed a level of cataclysm associated with polar shifts that was scientifically respectable in his own day (one of the major schools of 19th-century geology was called catastrophism), but suspect in ours. There is no paleontological evidence for the cataclysmic cycle he proposed, even if catastrophism is back in vogue as a possible explanation for the mass extinctions of the dinosaurs, or even the mass extinctions at the end of the Cambrian geological period.

[11] The assigning of angelic guardians of the planets is scarcely new to Burgoyne: his angels are the same as William Lilly's (1647). The specific match to Lilly may not be coincidental. One of the more spiritually inclined of the 19th-century British astrologers, R. J. Morrison, who wrote under the name Zadkiel, published an abridgement of Lilly's classic, *Christian Astrology*. Curiously, given Morrison's own interests, the abridgement did not contain the angelic names.

consistent with typical astrological presentations, but they were hardly the same old stuff. Burgoyne slanted all of the astrological material he presented for occult practice: what is the significance of this symbolism? What does it *mean*? This, I believe, is why Papus chose to rely as heavily on Burgoyne as he did, given that Papus clearly had alternative sources for his presentation.

Papus constructed his astrological work around Burgoyne's occult descriptions of the planets, signs, and houses, while connecting the dots, so to speak, with material taken from the contemporary French astrological literature. As a result, Papus' work adheres more closely to classical astrological method than the typical contemporary English language work.[12] Burgoyne in turn relied more obviously on the occultists who viewed astrology from the outside looking in, than on the contemporary British astrologers. It is this outsider perspective which may be responsible for Burgoyne's extremely perceptive vision of the psychological motivations of the signs and planets. We know from his work in the H. B. of L. that he was a practicing astrologer, in that he drew up astrological charts for his students and interpreted them.[13]

Despite the philosophical, doctrinal, and methodological disparity of his sources—or perhaps because of it—Papus' synthesis of astrology is in fact one of the more interesting introductory presentations of the art. It may not be the ideal presentation for the potential working astrologer, but for the reader who looks to astrology as a source of insight, inspiration, and background, it is virtually unsurpassed. We might also add that modern ideas about copyright and authorship

---

[12] The two English language exceptions are the Englishman A. J. Pearce, who collected antiquarian materials seriously, and the American Luke Broughton, who presented a ptolemaic approach in his astrology, and had the distinction of predicting the assassination of Abraham Lincoln in his Civil War era periodical, *Broughton's Planetary Reader*.

[13] See, for example, Godwin *et al.*, *The Hermetic Brotherhood of Luxor*, pp. 37–39.

were not current then: Papus felt free and justified in appropriating extensive passages from Burgoyne (with attribution, we hasten to add); contemporary practitioners would not do this. Before we go on to the text itself, a couple of notes are in order about the subsequent influence of Papus. I had mentioned that Papus followed a fashion in French astrology that glorified the scientific perspective. It is important to understand this position within the greater context of occultism, and its subsequent effect on astrology.

Throughout much of the time since the establishment of the clockwork universe as the primary model of reality, occultism has looked to science for ideas and analogies. This influence is one that science in turn generally denies, because "Science" would prefer to believe that occultism is irrational. Instead, it would be more correct to view Occultism as trans-rational: rationalism can be easily viewed as a useful system for training the mind, even if rationalism, itself, is not capable of discerning the highest mysteries.

In fact, in following this line of reasoning, scientific discoveries have long been a source of inspiration to occultists. I have already mentioned how the geological theories of catastrophism surely played a role in Mackey's conception of the dangers of pole shifts. Later in the century, it was occultists who embraced the Theory of Evolution, because the biological system was such a good analogy for the perceived spiritual system.

The problem with embracing science in this way is that science changes. This shift was characterized thoroughly by Thomas S. Kuhn in his landmark work, *The Structure of Scientific Revolutions.*[14] Known now as paradigm shifts, scientific theories exist in a slowly changing matrix of concepts. The problem is that most people believe that the beliefs of their own time are Absolute Truth. Scientific theories also

---

[14] Thomas S. Kuhn, *The Structure of Scientific Revolutions* (Chicago: University of Chicago Press, 1962, 1970).

fall into this belief. Consequently, when we examine Papus' carefully wrought "science," we may groan at some of the anachronisms. Similarly, if more dangerously, the raging sexism and racism of so many of the occult works of this period (not to mention the Anti-Semitism, a particular failing of Papus) reflect societal attitudes that nonetheless were enshrined as scientific "fact" because of dubious measurements of things such as cranial capacity.[15] In a contemporary context, we have seen the emergence of the connection between quantum physics and Eastern mysticism through such authors as Fritjof Capra. As was recently pointed out by Brad Marston, the particular theory in physics which Capra used to create this analogy has lost favor, yet the beat goes on . . .[16] One may posit that all such analogies based on quantum physics, field theory, and probably even chaos, are likewise liable to be left in the dust. Furthermore, in the wake of the successes of chemistry in the treatment of various mental conditions, one has to wonder of the long-term impact of these discoveries on psychology, which had presumed to treat what are now known to be chemical imbalances in a less than providential way.[17]

Thus, we may apply caveats to the marriage of scientific discoveries with occultism, but that does not mean we should abandon all such attempts. It was precisely through the application of the idea of rationalism that Papus and his occult contemporaries could inspire the next generation of French astrologers, who took astrology along two dramatic paths. The first, Henri Selva, was to go Back to the Future, as Selva brought forward the work of the great 17th-century French astrologer Jean Baptiste Morin (Morinus): the *Astrologia Gallica* (1661). While Morinus, himself, was quite

---

[15] For a fuller discussion of this unfortunate tendency in science, please see Gould, *The Mismeasure of Man* (New York: W. W. Norton, 1981).
[16] Brad Marston, Letter to the Editor in *Tricycle: The Buddhist Review*, V(1): 8–10, 1995.
[17] See Kramer, *Listening to Prozak* (New York: Viking, 1993).

an astrological innovator, his method was firmly rooted in the classical style. Selva's 1902 work was, in turn, picked up by Friedreich Schwickert (1857–1930) and Adolph Weiss (1889–1956), who brought it to the attention of German readers through their multi-volume *Baumsteine die Astrologie*. Weiss immigrated to South America to escape the Nazis; he in turn translated and revised the work into Spanish as *Astrologia Racional*,[18] where it remains one of the premier reference works for serious Spanish-speaking astrologers.

The other major stream of influence exerted by Papus *et al.*, was through the subsequent work of Paul Choisnard (1867–1930), who was one of the earliest astrologers to attempt to apply statistical techniques to astrology: he was one of the direct forerunners to the more modern work of Michel Gauquelin, and subsequently, Françoise Gauquelin. However, Choisnard's work was not limited to statistical studies: he also published a volume detailing and discussing Thomas Aquinus' views on astrology, and this work remains in print.

It is worth mentioning that the gap between astrologers and occultists who speak different languages has grown since Papus' time. In the United States there seems to be a long-standing prejudice against foreign language education. Few astrological works by foreign authors are translated.[19] Even where there is substantial transmission, the influence is often one way. We have seen with Morinus to Weiss how a French source was picked up by an Austrian, who translated it into German and Spanish. Similarly, one of the other major Spanish astrological references, the *Diccionario Astrologico*, is actually a translation of the Frenchman Henri Gouchon.[20] Scanning a bookstore in Italy reveals substantial titles trans-

---

[18] Editorial Kier, S. A.: Buenos Aires, 1946, 1965.
[19] Samuel Weiser, of course, provides notable exceptions through publishing the works of the Hubers and Karen Hamaker-Zondag. But how many Americans are even vaguely aware of the works of André Barbault, a giant among French astrologers, or Thomas Ring, who occupied similar stature among Germans?
[20] Luis Cárcamo, Ed.: Madrid, 1975, 1987.

lated from the French, fewer from English-language sources, and almost none from German. The Germans seem to have English translations, but little else. We remain fragmented.

Papus' astrological work may not go down in history as the most significant work in astrology, although it is a good introductory work. However, from our vantage point as practitioners as well as students of history, his overt borrowing of sources is useful, because it can clarify the processes of transmission of ideas in the complex period that was the late 19th century. We may further remark that, by borrowing from Burgoyne and the Continental astrological tradition, he produced a work which provides fresh insights to those raised in the English-speaking astrological tradition. Thus, the occult generalist has succeeded in teaching the astrological specialist a thing or two!

The translation presented here is not strictly literal: a word-for-word translation between most languages would be incomprehensible. I have maintained most of Papus' paragraph and sentence structure and changed allusions for comprehension's sake. I have footnoted those places where I believe that Papus erred, or where supplemental information has become available in the interim. I would like to thank Margaret M. Meister for reading the translation for comprehensibility, Diana K. Rosenberg for providing background information on fixed stars, and Batya Stark for information on the attribution of sacred stones and the twelve tribes of Israel.

—J. LEE LEHMAN, PH.D.

A WORD TO THE READER

WE MUST STUDY ASTROLOGY. The basis of scientific studies pursued in the ancient temples of Egypt, Chaldea, China, etc., was the survey of the sky. The march of the Sun through the twelve zodiacal signs formed the point of departure of a host of mythological histories (the Conquest of the golden Fleece, the Labors of Hercules).

The rising and setting of constellations, their multiple movements in the immense celestial sea, Maha Maria, kept the attention of the initiates and formed the basis of a teaching precise as well as deep. Even better, the alphabetic characters of the Egyptian hieroglyphs, Chaldean cuneiform and early Chinese* were in the shape of some constellations. See figure 1.

The sky thus becomes the conservatory of language, and if all the intellectual monuments of the Earth were destroyed, it would be sufficient to take a systematic survey of the sky in order to reconstitute the principles of linguistic construction. You can take the following:

Three circles of general construction;
the circle of the Central Star;
the circle of the Wandering Stars;
and the circle of the Fixed Stars;
Seven Wandering Stars (planets);
Twelve stationary signs (zodiac);

then represent it all by the hieroglyphic signs and you will have the key to all these alphabets consecrated with 22

---

* See *First Elements of Reading of the Egyptian language, of the Sanskrit language, of the Hebrew language*, by Papus.

Figure 1.   An early astrologer.

letters that the University of Babylon gave back exoterically around 500 B.C.E.

It is necessary, therefore, to know the first elements of astrology well in order to fruitfully study magic, alchemy, mythology, and the key to the myths of the Sacred Books.

In the present work we don't present the means of erecting a horoscope: this constitutes a practical exercise of the astrological science, and should be done by specialists more competent than ourselves.[1]

We want only to make all serious researchers recognize the techniques and terms employed by astrologers. Besides,

---

[1] The reader should also be aware that there are mail-order services, such as Astro Communications Services in San Diego, that specialize in generating horoscopes by computer. Tr.

we have attempted to integrate the ideas of astrologers with the planets and to assign to them some data from contemporary astronomy.[2] In order to increase the clarity of our exposition, we will use illustrations extensively. Every technical example is accompanied by an explanatory figure. We hope, as well, that this work will be considered under its real guise, as an introduction to the survey of the deeper works of astrologers and of ancient or modern hermeticians.

---

[2] In this light, we have supplemented Papus' astronomical discussions with information gleaned from the many planetary satellite programs, as well as data collected by other sources unavailable in his time, like the Hubble Telescope. Tr.

CHAPTER ONE

THE CELESTIAL SPHERE[†]

IN THE NIGHT IF WE DIRECT our regard toward the starry sky, we can see, if the weather is clear, an enormous quantity of stars, more or less brilliant, and so overwhelming that it seems impossible to even recognize anything at first. While observing all these brilliant points in the sky more closely, we begin to notice that some of them form distinct groups of stars separate from one another.[1]

How to Recognize these in the Mass of Stars

In antiquity, people formed these groups of stars, figures to which the imagination of the wise ones assigned some shapes. Some are merely geometric, but most often people used the shapes of animals, of people, or of objects. One gave the name of constellations to these clumps of stars, and there are some unique constellations in the Northern Hemisphere which are directly overhead in Europe, and some others unique to the Southern Hemisphere, on the other side the equator.

The Starry Route

One should also note, that besides some stationary stars that appear studded in the sky like so many lights, there are also mobile bodies that promenade through the constellations.

---

† Original footnotes to the text are presented with an asterisk. Translator's notes are cited as footnotes. Tr.

[1] The discussion is of asterisms and constellations. An asterism is a portion of a constellation which was recognizable as an entity.

These stars are first the Sun, then the Moon. Of the rest, the planets, we will speak later. Let us hold on, for the moment, to the exterior sensations that they produce on the Earth. We will see that a lot of obvious movements are actually due to the movement of the Earth, but we will ignore this at present, because it would interfere with the clarity of our descriptions. Therefore, in observing the sky, people realized that in its course the Sun traversed the constellations, always the same; they noted that the Moon followed the same course, as well as all the other wandering stars, or planets.

The Zodiac

This pathway followed by the celestial wanderers through the sky was called the way of the celestial animals, or the divine starry way, or zodiac. This zodiac is composed of twelve constellations, and this study is most important for the astronomer, as much as for the astrologer. We will return to it for more detail later.

Divisions of Sky

All the bodies in the sky therefore divide in two major types; first the stationary stars forming the constellations, then the wandering stars moving through the twelve constellations of the zodiac.

Stationary Stars

The word "fixed" applied to the stars is relative; these stars indeed don't displace individually, this is what differentiates them from the wandering stars. But the sky displaces around the Celestial Pole; behold why the ancients considered the sky like a large ocean, within which the constellations rose or set.

The Celestial Sphere

A set of astronomical observations ancient and modern based on the rising and setting of the constellations.

The Celestial Sphere
(According to the Ancient System of Ptolemy)

In order to navigate, people divided the celestial sphere in a very simple and analogous way to the division of the Earth. The celestial sphere has two Poles; a North or Arctic Pole, and a South or Antarctic Pole. Between these two Poles and in the middle of the sphere is the celestial Equator, parallel to the Poles; the zodiac, acting in the sky like the ecliptic on the Earth; cuts the Equator in two places, in such a way that six signs of zodiac are above the Equator, toward the North or Arctic Pole, and six beneath the Equator, toward the South or Antarctic Pole. The accompanying figure will clarify this situation of zodiac and Equator. (See figure 2 on page 4.)

The sign that is the most northern point of the zodiac is Cancer; the sign that is the most southern, closest to the Antarctic Pole, is Capricorn.

In addition to the equator and to the parallel circles in the celestial sphere, there is another circle that passes through Capricorn and is called the Tropic of Capricorn. (See figure 3 on page 6.)

The two signs of zodiac of which we have just spoken, Cancer and Capricorn, forming the extreme northerly point and the extreme southerly point of the zodiac, constitute the line of the solstices; two other signs, the eastern point (Aries), and the western point (Libra), constitute the line of the equinoxes.

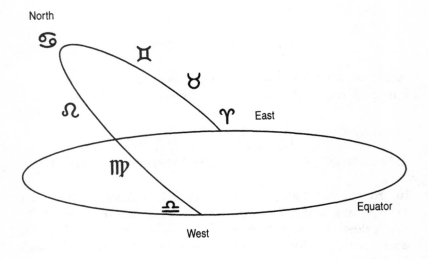

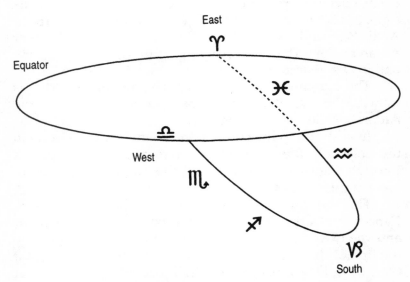

Figure 2.   The zodiac signs ascending and signs descending.

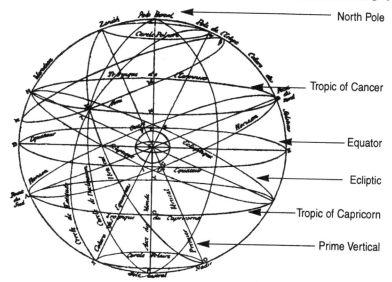

North Pole

Tropic of Cancer

Equator

Ecliptic

Tropic of Capricorn

Prime Vertical

Figure 3. The Tropic of Capricorn. This is a reproduction from the figure original to the French edition.

These last two signs are exactly placed at the two points where the zodiac cuts the equator. In the starry way, one finds, therefore, the grand celestial cross, defined by the line of the equinoxes and solstices, and constituted by four signs, North-South, and East-West; Cancer-Capricorn, and Aries-Libra.

The astrologers call these four signs, the angular houses, because they occupy the four angles of sky, or the four cardinal points. (See figure 4 on page 6.)

These four angles indicate the beginning of the four seasons. It is necessary now to memorize in order the names of the twelve zodiacal signs. These signs are the following, with the corresponding months, because the astrologers' year begins in March:

Aries (♈):   20 March . . . .   20 April
Taurus (♉):   20 April . . . .   20 May

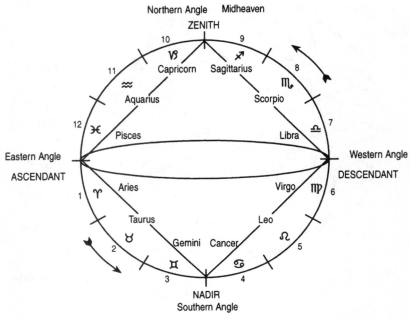

Figure 4.   The four angles of the chart: Ascendant, Nadir, Descendant, and Midheaven.

Gemini (♊):	21 May	20 June
Cancer (♋):	21 June	22 July
Leo (♌):	23 July	22 August
Virgo (♍):	23 August	22 September
Libra (♎):	23 September. . . .	22 October
Scorpio (♏):	23 October	21 November
Sagittarius (♐):	22 November. . . .	21 December
Capricorn (♑):	22 December	20 January
Aquarius (♒):	21 January	18 February
Pisces (♓):	19 February	19 March

These dates indicate the entrance of the Sun in the different signs in 1916.

In order to learn the signs of zodiac in sequence by heart, you may use the following mnemonic:

```
AR   — TAU  — GE
CAN  — LE   — VI
LIB  — SCOR — SAG
CAP  — AQU  — PI
```

In small doses, you will manage to memorize the succession of the signs of the zodiac, which is indispensable to memorize for astrological studies.

Each one of the twelve signs of zodiac is composed of groups of stars, which, united together, comprise geometrical figures. All of antiquity assigned to the zodiacal signs the symbolic figures of animals, personages, or objects who resemble their name. Finally, each one of the zodiacal signs is also given a glyph (see figure 4), and we enlist the reader to combine the glyph and the mnemonic formula above.

We will proceed, for the moment, but let's retain what we have learned concerning the zodiac, which will give us the opportunity to discuss it in greater detail later.

CHAPTER TWO

The Planets

THE ZODIAC IS THE ROAD followed by the planets or mobile stars. All the planets traverse successively through the twelve signs of the zodiac, but each one with a different speed. Let us take as our first example the march of the Sun, which served as the basis for the establishment of a mass of allegorical stories in ancient mythology.

We will give some elements of plain astronomy first, and it is only in a following chapter that we will bring back the astrological point of view in interpreting the physical data of the astronomers.

First Hierarchy of the Planets

For the astronomer, the Sun is at the center of our planetary world. (See figure 5, page 10.) If we move away from the position of the Sun, we have the planets in the following sequence:

1) Sun
2) Mercury
3) Venus
4) The Earth and the Moon
5) Mars
6) Multiple asteroids
7) Jupiter
8) Saturn
9) Uranus
10) Neptune
11) [Pluto]

We highly recommend the works of our master and friend Camille Flammarion to the serious student.[4]

Let's summarize the main elements in the following section.

---

[4] Flammarion's works have never been translated into English. Fortunately, there are many good introductory works in astrology in English which would provide excellent supplementary material.

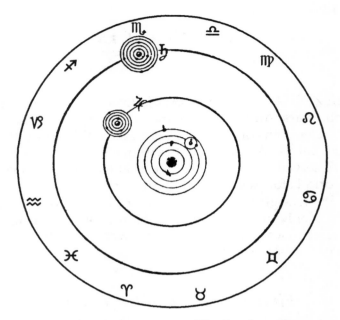

Figure 5.   Copernican system. The Sun is at the center.

The Sun

To all Lords, all honor.

The Sun is 108 times larger than the Earth, in diameter.[5]

The Sun's mass and volume follow some analogous connections.[6]

If the Earth is represented by a head of a pin, the Sun would be a small melon. One sees therefore the enormous mass of this star. For the observer of appearances, the Sun traverses

---

[5] The modern measurement of relative diameter is 108.97.
[6] Remembering that diameter or length is two dimensional, while volume is three dimensional.

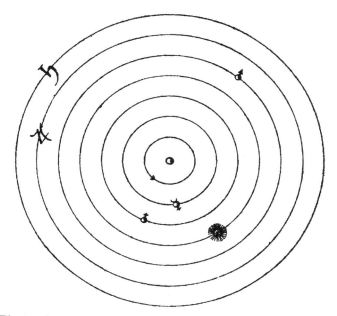

Figure 6. Ptolemaic system. The Earth is at the center.

the twelve signs of the zodiac in 365 days and a fraction (0.2564). It moves through a sign in approximately thirty terrestrial days. The Sun travels through a sign of zodiac every month and takes one year to take a tour of the zodiac and to return to its point of departure.

We may note in passing, that the Sun, at the end of the year, doesn't return precisely to the point where it was at the same time the previous year. At the spring equinox, for example, March 21st, the Sun reaches the equinoctial point some time before the same point of the previous year; as a result of precession of the equinoxes, of which we spoke in a previous survey.

Don't forget that it is the Earth which produces all these movements, but, once again, we argue from visual appearances in order to remain clear, when it involves these topics.

The ancients, who placed the Earth to the center of world (see figure 6) saw the Sun arrive March 21st at the beginning of the ascending signs of zodiac, the signs of Northern orientation from Aries to Cancer. In those days, they supposed that the Sun was the greatest force, and the source of all happiness. But let us not anticipate, but remain at present in astronomy and continue our elementary survey.

Mercury
Of all the known planets, it is closest to the Sun; Mercury finds itself always plunged into the solar rays. This planet, which is rarely visible to the naked eye, is the smallest planet and the most dense. Its diameter doesn't quite reach the half of diameter of the Earth.[7]

Venus
Venus is the most brilliant star of sky: its appearance surpasses the most beautiful stars. Venus is sometimes so vivid that the planet becomes visible in full daylight.[8]

Venus has close to the same diameter as that of Earth, but its density is a little weaker.[9] The planet is surrounded by an analogous atmosphere to the terrestrial atmosphere.[10]

The Earth
The Earth has the shape of a sphere flattened a little toward the two poles; it rotates from West to East in a uniform movement around an axis; it is the movement of rotation

---

[7] The radius is 0.383 that of Earth. Of course, we know much more about the astronomy of the planets than Papus, in great part because of our technology, the fly-bys of various satellites.

[8] We recommend that students observe these planets. Many newspapers carry sky maps, or at least a listing of what planets are visible in the evening. This information is also available on some astronomy web pages. Venus, under ideal conditions, is so bright that the ancients talked of the "horns" of Venus—the crescent Venus—in the same fashion that they discussed the "horns" of the Moon. It is thought by some that this is part of the connection of both planets to the zodiacal sign Taurus (the horned Bull)—as we shall see.

[9] The radius ratio is 0.9488.

[10] We know now that Venus' atmosphere is radically unlike that of Earth's: a planet upon which the Greenhouse Effect has run amok. The result is a surface temperature so high (mean temperature 482° C or 900° F) that it would melt lead or zinc.

that defines the length of day. The second movement is the revolution around the Sun, completely accomplished in one year or 365 days.

The great circle that one gets through cutting the surface of the Earth by a plane passing through the line of the poles (or the Earth's axis), is called the Meridian. The length of a terrestrial meridian[11] is 40,000 kilometers.[12] The radius of the Earth is 6,366 kilometers.[13]

Three-quarters of the Earth's surface is covered by the oceans; the other quarter contains the continents. The biggest area of land mass is situated in the hemisphere which would have Paris for the pole.

The continents are composed of plains, valleys, and mountains. The highest mountain, Mount Everest (Himalayas), has a height of 8,840 meters, that is to say a little more than a thousandth part of terrestrial radius. The unevenness of the Earth is proportionally less appreciable than that of an orange peel.

The deepest known depth in the ocean is 9,425 meters.[14]

The Moon

The Moon is a satellite of the Earth, that is to say, a smaller planet that revolves around the Earth while the Earth revolves around the Sun.

The radius of the Moon is about $3/11$ of the radius of Earth, and its volume is $1/50$ of the volume of Earth. The density of the Moon is $6/10$ of the density of the Earth. The mean distance of the Moon to the Earth is 60 terrestrial radiuses. The Moon accomplishes its revolution around the Earth in 27-$1/3$ days. The Moon goes around the Earth about thirteen times for one turn of the Earth around the Sun.

---

[11] i.e., the circumference.

[12] Satellite measurements give 40,075 km.

[13] Satellite version: 6378.14.

[14] This figure hasn't changed much. The deepest part of the oceans is in the Pacific, the Mindanao Deep at 10,918 m.

The solar inequalities are relatively more pronounced on the lunar globe than on the terrestrial globe.[15] There is no water on the lunar surface, nor substantial atmosphere. The effects of attraction of the Moon on the Earth are very appreciable and peak nearly twice a day in the phenomenon known as the tides.

Mars

This planet, of which the diameter is half that of the Earth, is distinguished by its very pronounced reddish hue. Mars has two satellites, Phobos and Deimos, discovered in 1877 by an American astronomer.[16] Mars has a volume seven times less than that of Earth.[17] On Mars, the days are nearly the same as ours.[18]

Multiple Asteroids or Minor Planets

Their revolutions around the Sun are between three and eight years. The first four, ranked by order of seniority of discovery, are: Ceres, Pallas, Juno and Vesta. One knows today of more than 800.[19]

Jupiter

Jupiter is the largest of the planets, the most brilliant after Venus. Its diameter is $\frac{1}{10}$ that of the Sun and exceeds the di-

---

[15] This means that the temperature range on the Moon is vastly greater than on the Earth.

[16] A. Hall.

[17] The volume figure is off. Since the other planets were compared by diameter or radius, we can give the equivalent measurement here: Mars' radius in 3,397.2 km, or 0.533 that of Earth. In Papus' day, it was still acceptable scientifically to assume life on Mars: the change in the appearance of Mars during the seasons resulted in the very logical theory that life was responsible. We know now that the changes are due to the melting and refreezing of the polar ice caps.

[18] 24.6229 hours.

[19] In 1996 we know of thousands of asteroids, including some whose orbits are completely outside of the traditional asteroid belt. For further information on this subject, the reader may consult my book, *The Ultimate Asteroid Book*, or a number of volumes by other writers.

ameter of the Earth by 11 times; its density is a little superior to that of water. This enormous globe completes a revolution in 10 hours or less.[20]

Jupiter is surrounded by eight moons.[21] The first four were discovered by Galileo in 1610; the fifth by Barnard in 1892; the last three were discovered from photographs in the period from 1904 to 1908. The eighth moves in a retrograde fashion.

Saturn

Saturn is the largest planet after Jupiter; its diameter is equivalent to nine times that of Earth, its density is less than that of water. Saturn is the lightest and the most flattened of all the planets.

The factor that distinguishes Saturn from the other planets is the large and thin ring which surrounds it at a distance from the planet; the ring's width is nearly equal to the diameter of the planet.[22] With a good lens one sees the ring split in two others, separated by an empty space which appears dark by contrast; a very powerful telescope makes out a further detail to the interior ring, with two other rings separated by a dark band.[23]

In 1656, Huygens discovered the existence of the ring that Galileo had seen for the first time in 1610, but without

---

[20] Jupiter is now classified as the first of the Gas Giants, also known as the Jovian planets. The inner portion of the Solar System is characterized by planets composed mainly of rock. From Jupiter through Neptune, the planets are composed of gases like carbon dioxide, nitrous oxide and methane, which are in the solid state because of the great cold.

[21] As a result of more intense telescopic study, as well as the fly-by of multiple satellites, the number of moons is now 16. In addition, Jupiter has a small ring similar in structure to Saturn's.

[22] We now know that the rings of Saturn are actually a very complex system of multiple rings; further, Jupiter and Uranus also have ring systems.

[23] Much more detail is now available, thanks in great part to the fly-bys of the two Voyager satellites. The reader is referred for further information to NASA's excellent publications, or, for those with Internet access, web pages such as "http://bang.lanl.gov/solarsys/solarsys.htm."

being able to distinguish its shape; the division into two distinct rings was discovered in 1663 by Cassini.

Saturn has ten satellites.[24] The ninth is very distant from the planet, and moves in a retrograde sense, that is to say in inverse direction of movement of the planet.

Uranus

This planet was discovered by Herschel in 1781. This great observer of the sky explored a region of the constellation Gemini with the goal of searching there for double stars; he saw a star with a very rounded contour that he took first to be a comet, but after having followed its movements over the course of years, recognized it as a new planet. Uranus' volume is 70 times that of Earth.

Uranus has four satellites who move in the retrograde direction.[25] The two more distant from the planet were discovered by Herschel in 1785, and the two other by Lassel in 1851.

Neptune

Its diameter is worth about four times that of Earth; it is an invisible planet to the naked eye. Neptune has a satellite that moves in the retrograde sense.[26] A young French astronomer [Urbain Jean Joseph] Le Verrier, discovered Neptune by mass calculation, and the discovery of this planet in 1846[27] caused a universal sensation.

This brief survey of the planets, from the astronomical point of view, allows us to return to our astrological survey.

We will study successively and synthesize the meanings of the diurnal and nocturnal domiciles of the planets,

---

[24] The current count (1996) for Saturn satellites is eighteen, with two to four more additional ones in preliminary observation.

[25] The current count is 15.

[26] Currently, a total of eight moons have been discovered.

[27] The actual first observations were by Johann Gottfried Galle of the Berlin Observatory, and Louis d'Arrest, an astronomy student.

their aspects of dignity or of fall, their respective positions, each with respect to the other, and we will complete this brief information with a detailed survey of the truly initiatory nature of the planets, according to the scholarly author of *The Light of Egypt*.[28]

We saw that the astronomers only concern themselves with the Exterior Sky. They study celestial anatomy. Astrologers claim to be able to describe the intimate life of every planet, its friends and enemies, its temperament, its place of strength, and the places where it loses strength; finally its physiology and psychology.

Astrologers also describe the character of each sign of the zodiac, and their connections with planets in a particular manner.

When a royal child was born, the astrologers attached to the court noted with care the position of every planet in each sign of the zodiac at the precise instant of the birth. The astrologer delineated, by this means, the meaning of the horoscope of the future sovereign, by calculating the strength or the weakness of each planet and the reactions of the signs and some constellations on these planets. One understands that astronomers, alarmed by these pretensions of the astrologers, have considered them like dreamers, and that astrologers, full of mercy for the elementary science of the astronomers, have considered them like black sheep and as profaners of the art.[29]

Our goal is to put the reader in the position to read either the old or modern astrologers without any other expectation.

Two fundamental remarks seem indispensable from the beginning. First: how many planets is it necessary to study in order to understand astrology? The ancient masters

---

[28] See Thomas Burgoyne, *The Light of Egypt*, published in 1889 by the Religio-Philosophical Publishing House, San Francisco. Reissued 1963 by H. O. Wagner, Denver, CO.

[29] This is a play on words in French. The word for black sheep (or outsider) is *profanes*, while the word for profaner is *profanateur*.

of the astrology used only seven planets: Saturn, Jupiter, Mars, the Sun, Venus, Mercury, and the Moon.

The modern astrologers, wanting to act scientifically, added Uranus and Neptune.[30] In my personal opinion, this is a gross mistake.

If we wanted to calculate the influence of every moving body of the heavens, it would be necessary to add the asteroids that orbit between Mars and Jupiter to the count[31]; astrology would become so complicated that all horoscopes would be impossible to prepare. It would be also necessary to take into account some of the comets.

The ancients had divided the sky in seven zones of influences, and while any zone may contain one or more stars, it didn't change the zone count. Uranus and Neptune must be considered to be in the zone of Saturn, as well as placing the asteroids in the zone of Jupiter. But we won't consider Uranus nor Neptune in our exposition.

For a clear understanding of astrology, we must begin, like small children, with the alphabet. Just as we gave a mnemonic method for the signs of zodiac, in the same way we will ask the reader to learn by heart the following mysterious sentence:

SA-JU-MA-SU-VE-ME-MO.

It is the order of the planets adopted by astrologers, according to the system of Claudius Ptolemy.

SATURN - JUPITER - MARS - SUN - MERCURY - VENUS - MOON.

It is necessary, therefore, first of all to learn this planetary order by heart in order to have the key to a whole series of astrological pictures.

---

[30] Pluto was not discovered until after Papus' death, but is treated the same way as Uranus and Neptune by most astrologers.
[31] We have already seen that there are many more possible orbits for the asteroids than given.

THE PLANETS ☽ 19

Every planet is, astrologically speaking, a character, having, in the heavens, a favorite place or domicile, also having some friends and some enemies among the other planets, all like the humans, being of good cheer when meeting a friend, and of bad disposition upon meeting an enemy (aspects), with a variety of moods depending on whether the friend or the enemy is far or near.

There are some multiple and complicated calculations, and from which one can realize the difficulty of a comprehensive survey of astrology, however urgently this study was pursued in all the temples of antiquity. Let's, therefore, proceed slowly and by stages.

Domiciles of the Planets

Every planet has two domiciles or rulerships, a diurnal (daytime) domicile, the other nocturnal domicile, except the Sun and the Moon who each have one domicile only.

Saturn has as diurnal rulership of Aquarius (eleventh sign of the zodiac) and nocturnal rulership of Capricorn (tenth sign of the zodiac).

Jupiter, day ruler of Pisces (twelfth sign of the zodiac), nocturnal rulership of Sagittarius (ninth sign of the zodiac).

Mars, diurnal ruler of Aries (first sign of the zodiac), nocturnal domicile of Scorpio (eighth sign).

The *Sun,* unique domicile Leo (fifth sign).

Venus, day domicile of Taurus (second sign), nocturnal of Libra (seventh sign).

Mercury, diurnal domicile Gemini (third sign), nocturnal domicile Virgo (sixth sign).

The *Moon,* unique domicile of Cancer (fourth sign).

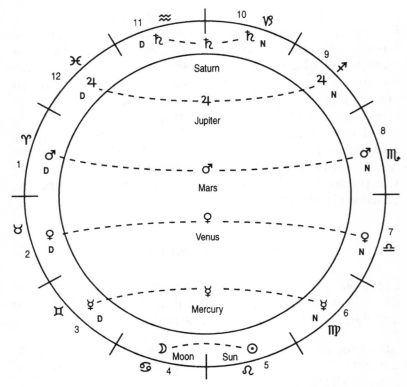

Figure 7. The glyphs for the planets and signs. N = Nocturnal; D = Diurnal.

Since this survey is critical in astrology, we give two figures: first, figure 7 is from the atlas of Dupuy which shows us the glyphs of the planets and the signs. And second, figure 8, which is a circular figure that illustrates the distinctive connections.

This question of the seven astrologically important planets, necessarily presents us with another difficulty: the astrologers place the zodiac with the North at the bottom, the South at the top, following with East on the left and West on the right.

In the astronomical zodiac, the Sun leaves the Orient (East), goes up toward the North, and redescends toward the

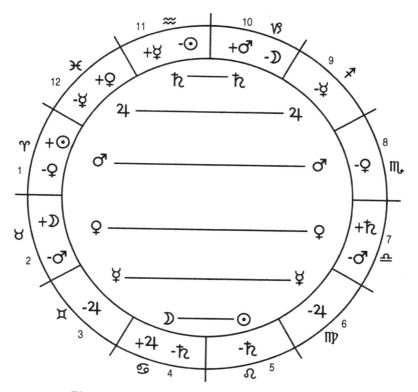

Figure 8. The connections between the signs.

South, as it seems clear to the ordinary observer. Astrologers, by contrast, put Aries on the left and Libra on the right, and the path of the Sun goes from left to right in descending.

These remarks made, we will leave their habits to the astrologers and will imagine the signs as they were seen during all antiquity.

Dignities and Detriments of the Planets

Besides their domicile (rulership), the planets have some zodiacal placements where they are in dignity, honored, and some others where they are constrained and, in astrological terminology, Detriment, or Fall (Exile). It is important to retain this new status of every planet. (See Table 1 on page 23.)

From now on, these ideas of Exaltation, Detriment, and Fall will prove useful to determine for every zodiacal sign at the time of analysis. The key to these dignities and debilities is easy.

1. The signs in opposition to the signs where the planets have their diurnal or nocturnal rulerships constitute the place of *Detriment* of these planets.

2. The signs in opposition with the place of *Exaltation* gives the *Fall*.

In order to understand the ancient astrologers, it is necessary take into account the following items:

1. The 18th degree of Gemini through the 12th degree of Cancer exercises the influence of the *Combust Way* (*Via Combusta*), which antagonizes favorable influences and increases the bad.[32]

2. The first to the 10th degree of Libra and 11th to the 30th degree of Sagittarius, exercises the influence of the Head of the Dragon (North Node).[33]

3. The 30 degrees of Virgo, the degrees 11 to 30 of Libra, 11 to 20 of Scorpio and 1 to 10 of Sagittarius are influenced by the Tail of the Dragon (South Node).[34]

---

[32] The normal definition of the *Via Combusta* is 15 Libra through 15 Scorpio.

[33] This is considered to be a beneficial placement. However, this allocation of degrees is not standard.

[34] This is considered a malefic placement. However, this allocation of degrees is not standard.

Table 1. Dignities and Detriments.

PLANET	EXALTATION	DETRIMENT	FALL
Saturn	Libra	Cancer and Leo	Aries
Jupiter	Cancer	Gemini and Virgo	Capricorn
Mars	Capricorn	Taurus, Libra	Cancer
Sun	Aries	Aquarius	Libra
Venus	Pisces	Aries	Virgo
Mercury	Virgo	Sagittarius, Pisces	Pisces
Moon	Taurus	Capricorn	Scorpio

The Planets

Here, remaining, the tables of the planetary dignities and debilities who will inform this topic. [Modern astrologers tend to follow Lilly. See Appendix, page 125–126, for tables used today. Tr. note.]

Planetary [Essential and Accidental] Dignities

All planets free of the Combust Way receive 5 points of dignity.

If *Saturn, Jupiter,* and *Mars* are Oriental with regard to the Sun,[35] they receive 2 points of dignity.

If *Venus* and *Mercury* are Occidental with regard to the Sun,[36] they receive 2 degrees of dignity.

The waxing *Moon,* that is to say since the 1st until the 15th day of its monthly evolution, receives 2 points of dignity.

---

[35] i.e., they rise before the Sun in the sky.
[36] i.e., they rise after the Sun.

All planets in their signs of rulership, diurnal or nocturnal, or in reception, receive 5 points of dignity.

All planets in their sign of Exaltation receive 4 points of dignity.

All planets in Triplicity receive 3 points of dignity.

All planets in the 1st or 10th houses receive 5 points of dignity.

All planets in the 4th, 7th, or 11th houses receive 4 points of dignity.

All planets in the 2nd or 5th houses receive 3 points of dignity.

All planets in the 9th house receive 2 points of dignity.

All planets in the 3rd house receive 1 point of dignity.

All planets in conjunction with *Jupiter* or *Venus* receive 5 points of dignity.

All planets in trine aspect with *Jupiter* or *Venus* receive 4 points of dignity.

All planets in sextile aspect with *Jupiter* or *Venus* receive 3 points of dignity.

All planets in conjunction, sextile or trine with the four Royal Stars receive 6 points of dignity.[37]

All *combust* planets receive 5 points of debility.[38]

---

[37] Generally, only the conjunctions are used. The royal stars (and their 1950 positions) are Aldebaran (9 Gemini), Regulus (29 Leo), Antares (9 Sagittarius) and Fomalhaut (3 Pisces). Most other lists also include Spica (23 Libra) as the fixed star with the most dignity.

[38] The points of debility are generally expressed as negative points; thus, a combust planet is given -5 points of dignity. A combust planet was considered debilitated because the light of the Sun prevented the planet from being seen.

All planets who are Under the *Sun's* Beams, that is to say, in the sign that the Sun has just cleared, receive 4 points of debility.[39]

If *Saturn, Jupiter* and *Mars* are Occidental with regard to the *Sun*,[40] they receive 2 points of debility.

If *Venus* and *Mercury* are oriental with regard to the Sun, they receive 2 points of debility.

The waning *Moon*, that is to say from the 15th day of its monthly evolution up to next New Moon, gets 2 points of debility.

All planets in the sign of their Detriment get 5 points of debility.

All planets in the sign of their Fall get 4 points of debility.

All planets in a position lacking any essential dignity are called *peregrine*, and receive 5 points of debility.[41]

All planets in the 12th house receive 5 points of debility.

---

[39] This is a variant definition. The usual definition for Under the Sun's Beams is the region from 8 to 17 degrees ahead of or behind the Sun. The reason behind this definition is that when a planet is Under Beams, it can sometimes be seen, but only under the most ideal weather conditions, and if the planet itself is quite bright. Thus, Venus can be seen more frequently Under Beams than Mercury, because Venus appears brighter in the sky.

[40] Normally, the expression would be "Mars is Occidental"; the reference to the Sun is assumed.

[41] There are two classical definitions plus a variant to the concept of lacking all essential dignity. The definition which Papus is following here is actually that of Morinus (Jean Baptiste Morin, 17th century), who simplified the definition by only using the so-called major or strong essential dignities: the earlier definition was to also include the minor dignities, *Term* and *Face*. Papus gives the Faces under the heading "Decans," but does not call them an essential dignity. The variant concerns whether a planet can be considered peregrine if it is in mutual reception. For more information on this topic, see my books, *Essential Dignities* (1989) and *Classical Astrology for Modern Living* (1996) published by Whitford Press.

All planets in the 6th or 8th house receive 4 points of debility.

All planets in conjunction with *Saturn* or *Mars* receive 5 points of debility.

All planets in square aspect to *Saturn* or *Mars* receive 3 points of debility.

All planets in opposition to *Saturn* or *Mars* receive 4 points of debility.

The Planetary Aspects

The planets promenade in the sky. They meet, cross, and exchange some good or bad influences between them, depending on whether they are good or bad together. There follows the study of the positions of the planets vis-a-vis each other, also known as the planetary aspects.

These aspects are studied by astronomers as well as astrologers. Astronomers see them only as physical phenomena, whereas astrologers teach that the diverse aspects of the planets have a very big influence on terrestrial beings and on political events.

In order to understand the planetary aspects, it suffices to divide the sky into degrees, like astronomers. One can establish the connection of the angles with the astrological houses then, by remembering that a house has 30 degrees.[42]

When the two planets are placed precisely together in

---

[42] There are two major kinds of house systems: the one referred to here is Equal House, in which by definition all houses are 30 degrees in size. Historically, the most common equal house systems began at either the beginning of the sign of the Ascendant, or at the Ascendant, itself. Another analogous system began at either the beginning of the sign of the Part of Fortune, or at the Part of Fortune, itself. The most common forms of house division today are unequal house systems, which place the Ascendant at the 1st house, and the Midheaven at the 10th, with varying methods for calculating the intermediate house cusps. Even if unequal houses are

the sky, the angle formed is zero degrees and it is called a conjunction.

When the planets are placed to the two extremities of sky, the one at noon and the other to the north,[43] for the astronomer the angle is 180 degrees, and for the astrologer it encompasses six houses (6 times 30° = 180°): it is the opposition between the conjunction and the opposition. The main aspects are the following:

Semi-sextile	30°	One house
Semi-square	45°	A house and a half
Sextile	60°	Two houses
Square	90°	Three houses
Trine	120°	Four houses
Sesquiquadrate	135°	Four houses and a half
Quincunx	150°	Five houses
Opposition	180°	Six houses

An easy way to remember the theory of the planetary aspects is to merely consider your watch. Imagine that each of the hands on your watch represents a planet, and you are going to understand successively all the planetary aspects.

When the big hand is at the twelve and the small hand is at the six, there is an opposition with the distance between the two hands of six divisions of dial or hours, which corresponds on the horoscope to six houses.

When the hands mark 1 o'clock, the big hand is on the twelve and the small on 1 hour; there is a house distance that represents the semi-sextile aspect.

If the small hand is between 1 hour and 2 and the big hand is on noon this gives the semi-square (45°).[44]

Two o'clock gives the sextile aspect (two houses).

used, it is true that the "average" house contains 30 degrees. Greater variations from 30 degrees occur with increasing terrestrial latitude.
[43] i.e., at midnight.
[44] This does not represent a real time, of course.

Three o'clock is the picture of the square (three houses), a quarter of the circle.

Four o'clock represents the trine (four houses), a third of the circle.[45]

Five o'clock represents the quincunx (150°).

Finally, 6 o'clock, the opposition.

To return to this demonstration of the figures of the aspects that we have given, it is sufficient to consider the times of 6:00 A.M. or of 6:00 P.M. to noon (or to midnight).

Noon less the quarter gives the square.

Noon less twenty, the trine, also called trigon[46] (120° or the third of the circle), etc., etc.

Remark on the Planetary Aspects

Trine and sextile are benefic aspects. Opposition and square are malefic aspects. Conjunctions are benefic if with Venus or Jupiter, malefic if with Mars or Saturn.

Jupiter and Venus are very good in conjunction, trine, or sextile.

The Sun, the Moon, and Mercury are doubtful in opposition and square, good in trine and sextile. See figure 9.

In the preceding pages, the reader has had the chance to get used to the idea, perhaps new, that the stars are living beings, as living as animals and plants; that the stars have friendships or hatreds, and influence one another by the fluid which circulates between them.[47]

---

[45] Note: Papus attributed the quincunx to being a third of the circle, which is incorrect.

[46] The use of "trigon" in English is less frequent than in French, but not unknown.

[47] When Papus was writing, physics still supported the theory of the ether, a ubiquitous "fluid" matrix which was the ground of being for all matter. Experiments by Albert A. Michelson and Edward Morley in 1881 cast doubt on the existence of ether. Finally, Einstein, in 1905, was able to fully resolve the issue by the theory of special relativity, which negated the necessity of an ether in order to explain the propagation of waves. Unfortunately, not all hermeticians keep up with physics in the propagation of their physical theories.

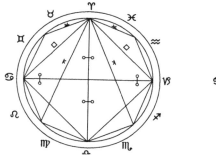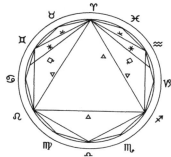

Figure 9. Left: The angular aspects of malefic rays (semi-square or 45°, square or 90°, sesquiquadrate or 135°, the opposition or 180°). Right: the angular aspects of benefic rays (semi-sextile or 30°, the sextile or 60°, the quintile or 72°, and the trine or 120°). Redrawn from the original.

The astrologer populates the sky with living beings and intelligent forces, whereas astronomy shows us only an immense cemetery of inert masses and of blind force.

The reading and the study of the following pages in which a grand initiate studies these planetary beings to the quadruple point of view: kabbalistically, astrologically, intellectually, and physically, will allow us to form a really true and profound idea of our topic.

The Planet Saturn[48]

Old Father Time, with his skeleton-like form and deathly scythe, is doubtless, well known to most of our readers. This is one of the many forms assumed by Saturn in his symbolical aspect. With the ancient Greeks he

---

[48] Rather than translate this extensive quotation from Thomas Burgoyne, I have inserted the text in the original English from the fifth edition of *Light of Egypt*, chapter VII, pages 258–270 respectively. Material from *Light of Egypt* is set off with a rule so readers can readily identify this quoted material.

Figure 10.   Saturn.

was known as Kronos, holding the cycle of necessity and eternity in one hand, and the symbol of death in the other; thus typifying eternal change of form, sphere, and function. Among the ancient Hebrews, Saturn was called Shebo, a name that literally means seven. It is composed of Ash-sheb, which means the star of old age; thus expressing the symbol of this planet.

Kabbalistically, the planet Saturn signifies silent meditation, and thus corresponds to the auricular attributes of the grand man; and, therefore, represents the senses and powers of hearing, listening, etc., within the constitution of humanity. We see, therefore, the mystical significance of the Kabbalistical conception of this orb, as silent meditation. In order to meditate, there must be silence; hence listening, hearing. Meditation is but the listening of the mind to the inspirations of the soul. Upon the esoteric planisphere, Saturn becomes the angel Cassiel, the genius of reflection in the astral light. It also presents to us the occult side of all theological mysteries; hence the medieval conception of this planet as the isolated hermit. It is in this sense, that, we find it symbolized in the Tarot; a system worthy of greater attention than seems to be paid to it by modern students of occult science.

Astrologically considered, the planet Saturn may be truthfully said to be the most potent and malignant of all the planets. This is not so much on account of the marked character of his influence, as the imperceptible, subtle manner, in which his influx undermines the vitality of the physical organism of those it afflicts. Mars comes like a thunderclap, and gives everyone to understand that there is something decidedly wrong. But Saturn is exactly the reverse. His nature is slow and patient, cunning and stealthy. At least, a good half of our world's suffering is due to the action of this planet; and in fact, nine-tenths of the ills of human life are due to the malignant rays of Mars and Saturn combined. Mars commits crime in a passionate and unthinking manner, and very seldom indeed is guilty of premeditated wrong. Saturn is the reverse. He thinks over all his plans very carefully before he attempts to put them into execution, and seldom makes a mistake.

Upon the Intellectual Plane, Saturn governs the higher group of the selfish sentiments, and the whole of the reflective qualities. Those dominated by his influx are retired, reserved, slow in speech and action. They express the highest form of reflection; consequently, they are studious, scientific and close reasoners. They generally tend to exclusiveness; hence, the hermit is a true type of this planet's action. They excel in all Occult studies.

Upon the Physical Plane, the only good that Saturn can do, is to strengthen the mentality, cool the passions, and make the native selfish and careful of his especial interests. When a person can claim these favors, he is exceedingly fortunate; because almost every aspect and position of this planet is rather more of a misfortune than a blessing. In nature it is cold and selfish, and is very apt to create a miserly disposition.[49]

---

[49] Burgoyne continues (but Papus does not): "If located in the mid-heaven, it brings ultimate ruin and disgrace. The horoscopes of Napoleon I and Napoleon III are splendid examples of this position. Both were born with Saturn in the M.C."

The Planet Jupiter

Under its symbolical aspect, we find Jupiter universally recognized among the ancient Greeks as Jove, the celestial father of all. Under the remoter Aryan symbolism, we find it represented as the 'All father of Heaven.' Both conceptions, Greek and Aryan, are identical. In the rude conceptions of the hardy sons of the north, we see the planet Jupiter depicted as Thor, from which comes the Saxon Thors-day and the modern English Thursday, the day over which the planet was supposed to rule.

Kabbalistically, the planet Jupiter signifies ethereal absorption within the grand man.[50] It therefore represents the power of scent or smell within the body of humanity. It is the sense by means of which the developed soul perceives and partakes the finer aromatic essences of Nature. Upon the esoteric planisphere, Jupiter becomes transformed into the celestial Zachariel or Zadkiel, and thus represents the impartial spirit of disinterestedness. In this capacity, it signifies the principles and philosophy of arbitration; the perfect adjustment of equilibrium by the withdrawal of disturbing forces. As symbolical of the attributes of ethereal absorption, we are frequently reminded of this planet by the Kabbalistical writers, of the books of Moses, who intimate that 'a

---

(mid cusp) and both attained to heights of fame, and then suffered from disgrace, and died in exile. [*Translator's Note:* This was also the configuration found in Hitler's chart.] When Saturn is exactly upon the zenith and afflicting the sun and moon, the child then born will not live twelve months. If in the ascendant, it makes the person timid and miserly, and generally produces a weak circulation. If in the 7th house, the native may expect a miserable life when he marries. When in the 5th house, the children of the native seldom live, unless one of the horoscopes, especially the wife's, counteracts this. The chief thing to note is whether the planet is well aspected or dignified. If such is the case, the native is much superior, and the influence is chiefly upon the mental plane. The native of Saturn is a thin, spare, lanky person; small, sharp eyes and black hair; and inclined to melancholy."
[50] The Grand Man, in Burgoyne's parlance, was the same as the Cosmic Human, the spiritual Adam, the archtype of the spiritual Man.

Figure 11. Jupiter.

sweet smelling savor' was acceptable to the Lord during the sacred rites of the temple service.

Astrologically considered, the planet Jupiter is the largest, and next to Saturn the most potent planet in our solar system. He signifies all that is truly good and charitable in human life. His action is truly noble, far removed from the sheepish timidity of Saturn, or the impudent forwardness of Mars. The genuine son of Jupiter fills the atmosphere around him with genial warmth. His soul is brimming full of honest good nature. Utterly incapable of practicing fraud himself, he never suspects it in others; hence, often becomes the victim of others' schemes and duplicity. This planet's nature suggests itself, when we say that, he takes every man to be honest until he is proven to be a rogue; and when this is proved, will forgive him once or twice before punishing him.

Upon the Intellectual Plane, Jupiter signifies the higher moral nature, the humanitarian qualities, and is the author of all noble and charitable institutions and enterprises. Those dominated by his influx express the highest form of human nature. There is something truly royal in this planet's influence, a mixture of the father, patriarch, and king. Such natives do much to redeem mankind from their general depravity. There will always be found in the natives of Jupiter, upon the intellectual plane, a fine sense of discrimination; hence, they possess rare qualities of justice, which entitle them to be judges of the people. When they err, it is always on the side of mercy.

Upon the Physical Plane, Jupiter may be called the greater fortune, when he rules over a nativity. He gives a sober, manly, commanding presence. The native is sober and grave in his speech, but, at the same time kind and sympathetic.[51]

The Planet Mars

This planet, of all others, in its symbolical aspect, was the object of divine honors in the eyes of the ancient world. Mars seems to have been the most sincerely worshipped, of all the gods, by our northern ancestors. The greatest glory, in their rude times, was enjoyed by the greatest warrior. Hence Mars, in his universal character, represented the god of war. He was also symbol-

---

[51] Burgoyne continues (but Papus does not): "If well dignified, he makes the native sincere, honest, and faithful; generous, liberal, prudent, and aspiring; strongly given to religion and moral sentiments; and generally speaking, all that can be desired, where morality, integrity, and faithful service is required. Located in the 2nd house, and well aspected, he confers the highest honor upon the native. Such persons always attain unto very important and responsible positions, which they fill with dignity to themselves, and honor to those who promote them. This planet's position, unafflicted in the 7th house, confers great matrimonial felicity; in the 11th house, faithful and powerful friends; in the 5th house, great gain and benefit through his offspring. But, when Jupiter is afflicted and ill dignified, then his nature is altered. The native is generally a pretender to all these noble qualities. He externally simulates them, but at heart, he is a shallow, scheming hypocrite, a wolf in sheep's clothing. He is the judge who renders his opinion according to the price. He is hollow, a fraud and a sham. The Jupiter man is generally a tall, well made, rather fleshy, generous looking, dignified person, sanguine complexion and brown hair."

ized as Vulcan, the celestial blacksmith, who forged the thunderbolts of Jove. This indicates the rule of Mars over iron, steel, fire, and edged tools.

Kabbalistically, the planet Mars signifies alimentiveness within the grand man, and therefore, represents the sense of taste in the human constitution. We have a direct reference to the expression of these martial forces in reference to the physical sensations in the New Testament, viz.: 'eat, drink and be merry, for tomorrow we die.' Upon the esoteric planisphere, Mars becomes transformed into the angel Samael (Zamael), wherein are shown the highest attributes of this spirit. As such, it represents the power and ability to appreciate the higher, finer, and more ethereal essences of the life wave, and therefore, to have domination over the powers of absorption and assimilation.

Astrologically considered, Mars typifies and embodies, in his astral expression, the spirit of cruelty, bloodshed, and of indiscriminate destruction. The true son of Mars is a genuine pugilist of the first water, and is never so happy as when thoroughly engaged in the vanquishing of his opponent. A type of this questionable spirit of enterprise may be found in the history of Great Britain. England is ruled by the sign Aries, the chief sign of Mars, and the typical Englishman is a Mars man. No better subject for study can be found to illustrate Mars, than John Bull. He is always fighting some one, and his past history for a thousand years upon land and sea, is the record of brilliant victories with very, very few reverses.

Upon the Intellectual Plane, Mars represents the spirit of enterprise, energy, and courage. Without a spice of this orb all men would be shiftless, effeminate cowards. Those dominated by the Martial influx are mechanical in the highest degree; and possess an unconquerable, untiring energy, and potent will.

Figure 12. Mars.

Upon the Physical Plane, Mars signifies all those who are in any Way engaged in the production of iron and steel. All Martial men prefer some business where sharp instruments, iron or fire are used, as is the case of butchers, barbers, blacksmiths, etc. . . .[52] When we compare the native of Mars with that of Saturn, we find them as polar opposites. The latter is like a low, lingering consumptive disease, and the former like a raging fever. No matter who or what they may be, depend on it, you will always find the native of Mars fiery, headstrong, furious in temper, and in respects cruel and destructive; and yet withal, they are generous to excess with their friends, and fond of good company. The general description of a true Mars man is somewhat as follows: medium height, strong, well made body, ruddy

---

[52] Burgoyne continues (but Papus does not): "When the planet is rising at birth, it always imparts a certain kind of ruddiness, either upon the face or hair, a fiery look, and gives to the native a dauntless, manly, appearance. If located in the second angle, it causes the native to become improvident and to spend money thoughtlessly. Such a person never becomes wealthy, but always lives up to his means. Located in the 10th house or mid-heaven, it never fails to cause the native much suffering from slander and consequent detriment of character."

complexion, piercing eyes, square set jaw, bold deter-
mined look, and quick, quarrelsome temper. The color
of the hair is variable, but it has generally a fiery tinge.

The Sun

The symbolical aspect of the glorious orb of day, un-
doubtedly, first occupied the attention, veneration, and
worship, of the primitive races of mankind. Every thing
in Nature depends absolutely upon the presence, and
kindly support of the shining sun, for its existence and
life. The literal interpretation of the Hebrew name for
the sun, Ashahed, is 'the all bountiful fire'; which is perfectly in harmony with the solar orb.

It is utterly impossible, in the brief space at our
command, to give even the remotest conception of the
innumerable ramifications connected with the various
mythologies which typify the sun. We will, therefore,
only add that Osiris of Egypt, Krishna of India, Belus of
Chaldea, and Ormazd of Persia, are merely different
personifications of the sun.

Kabbalistically, the Sun represents the central spiritual source of all. It is the divine Ego[53] of the grand man,
and therefore, signifies the spiritual potentialities of
creative power. It is the great I AM of all things; both
spiritual and temporal; and is, in itself, the grand conservatory of Life, Light and Love. Upon the esoteric
planisphere, the Sun becomes the great archangel
Michael, who defeats Satan and tramples upon the head
of the serpent of matter; and thenceforward, guards the
way of life and immortality, with the flaming swords of

---

[53] Please note, Burgoyne was writing this prior to the popularization of psychology, so his use of the word "ego" must be taken without its psychological trap-
pings. Philosophically speaking, the ego was the tri-partate person, consisting of
body, mind, and spirit.

Figure 13. The Sun.

solar power. In this sense the sun represents the positive, aggressive, controlling forces of the cosmos, as the forces of the sun are electric.

Astrologically considered, the Sun constitutes the central life principle of all physical things. His influx determines the absolute measure of physical vitality within each human organism. When the solar ray is not vitiated by the discordant configurations of malefic stars, the individual then born, will enjoy a sound constitution; more especially so, if the sun at the moment of birth is between the ascendant and meridian; or, in other words, during the increase of the diurnal sunshine, which is from sunrise to noon.

Upon the Intellectual Plane, the Sun governs the higher group of the selfish sentiments and lower group of moral qualities; the former, represented by firmness and self esteem, and the latter, by hope and conscientiousness. Those dominated by this influx are the natural born leaders of mankind. By their high-minded presence, they proclaim their 'right divine to govern.' They are proud and ambitious, yet magnanimous and noble. Hating all mean, petty and sordid actions, they

express the very highest form of true dignified man-
hood.

Upon the Physical Plane, the position of the sun in
the horoscope is one of vital importance; for on this, in
a male natus, hangs the vital thread of life. If evil rays
concentrate thereon; the life will be of short duration;
unless counteracting aspects intervene.[54]

The Planet Venus

In her mythological and symbolical aspect, the planet
Venus has been venerated, the wide world over, in her
dual character of Love and Wisdom. The bright star of
the morning, proud Lucifer, was the harbinger and genius of wisdom; and truly, none of the stars of heaven
can compare with the brilliance and glory of Venus
when she shines as the herald of day. As the goddess of
Love she is equally prominent. The ancient Greeks also
represented her as Aphrodite, wearing the horns of her
sacred Bull, Taurus.

Kabbalistically, the planet Venus signifies the Love
element within the soul, of the grand archetypal man;
and therefore, represents the sense of feeling within embodied humanity. It consequently expresses the clinging,
yielding, feminine portion of the human constitution.
Upon the esoteric planisphere, Venus becomes the celestial Anael, prince of the astral light. In this character we

---

[54] Burgoyne continues (though Papus does not): "When the sun is afflicted at birth,
his influence upon the native through life, will be malefic. When this is so; even
minor directions to the sun and moon combined, will bring about destruction of life;
the nature of which will be similar to that of the afflicting planets. And note this: for
prosperity and success in life; it is essential that the luminaries be well aspected and
favorably situated in the celestial figure. When the sun and the moon are afflicted at
birth, depend upon it, that person will have a very hard struggle against an adverse
fate all the days of his life; and it will not require the powers of an inspired prophet
to foretell his general destiny. 'From evil, discord and suffering are born.' "

Figure 14.   Venus.

behold her powers of transformation, and the 'conservation of forces.' As Isis represents the astral fluid in a state
of rest, pregnant (by the Holy Ghost) with the things TO
BE, Anael represents the same fluid in action. Therefore,
the Moon and Venus form the kabbalistic symbols for
the two modes of motion within the soul of the universe.

Astrologically considered, the planet Venus may
be said to represent mirth, joy, conviviality, as the influx
inclines those under her rule to pleasure-seeking, and
grand display. The pleasures of society are especially
governed by Venus. Balls, parties, concerts, and recep-
tions, possess irresistible attraction to those born under
her influence. If afflicted in a feminine horoscope, without strong counteracting rays, the native becomes 'unfortunate' and suffers from the loss of virtue, hence the
position of Venus is very important.

Upon the Intellectual Plane, Venus controls the
higher group of the domestic qualities, and also the
ideal, artistic, and musical, sentiments. Those dominated
by her influx excel in music, art and poetry, and become
noted for their refined accomplishments. But, at the
same time, they lack true moral power. They are guided

impulsively by their sentiments, passions and desires. Reason is conspicuous by its absence when their desires are aroused. Hence, the danger of being misled by flattery and sentimental nonsense is very great, when Venus is not protected by harmonious rays.

Upon the Physical Plane, when Venus has chief dominion over the mind of the native; she induces a strong predilection for society, and inclines to dancing, music, drawing, etc. She also confers a good humored, witty, kind and charitable disposition. Men dominated by this influx are always great favorites with the fair sex; but they are thoroughly deficient in firmness and self-control; and, if ill dignified, the male native will often find himself in awkward affairs; and is liable to fall into intemperance.[55, 56]

The Planet Mercury

In its symbolical aspect, the planet Mercury was most prominent as 'the messenger of the gods.' A thousand myths have been elaborated regarding 'the fleet-footed

---

[55] The French word chosen to translate "intemperance" was *la débauche*, which is completely similar in meaning to its cognate, "debauched." Thus, the French version conveyed a considerably stronger meaning here, one far more in keeping with the traditional meaning of an afflicted Venus than mere "intemperance."

[56] Burgoyne continued (but Papus did not): "A friendly aspect of Saturn in such cases would do much towards cooling and steadying the native's character and inducing reflection. Women born with Venus in the ascendant generally display the most amiable, engaging and fascinating qualities. If well aspected, they are neat and artistic in their dress and personal appearance, elegant in their homes and generally as virtuous as they are beautiful. It has been truly said, 'The general disposition derived from Venus is that of mildness and genuine good nature; and whatever defects may fall to the lot of the native, they are seldom great ones; and are more the results of weakness and a strong animal nature, than constitutional wickedness or a desire to do wrong.' In this we fully concur, and will only add that the chances to do wrong are multiplied by a prepossessing externalism. They are of medium stature, of a fair complexion, bright sparkling wicked eyes, handsome features and beautiful form."

Figure 15.   Mercury.

Mercury.' In the fertile imaginations of the early Greeks, the spirit of Mercury was ever on the alert to manifest its powers. His actions though sometimes mischievous, were often beneficial. It seems that the central idea of these ancients was to typify or express in external form the restless activities of the mercurial mind; hence, wings were placed upon his head and feet.

Kabbalistically, the planet Mercury signifies perception, and therefore, represents the power of sight within the grand body of the celestial man. It is the active power of self-consciousness within humanity, and the ability to see, perceive and reason. Upon the esoteric planisphere, Mercury becomes transformed into the angelic Raphael, the genius of wisdom and art. We see, therefore, that the esoteric forces of this orb are those which tend to elevate mankind from the animal planes to those of the human.

Astrologically considered, the influx of Mercury is mental and restless. No system of mere human invention would have dedicated to an almost invisible star; the least and most insignificant of all primary planets; the government of man's intellectual nature. Any fanciful system would have attributed such an important group of mental qualities to the Sun, or to the lordly Jupiter. The experience of the ancients, however, showed them that, neither the Sun nor Jupiter possessed any such influence; and it is upon the experience of ages, that the truths of astrology are founded; and the rules made for their application.

The qualities of Mercury may be well expressed by the American phrase, 'get up and get'; for energy, intellect, and impudence, constitute the chief characteristics of the purely Mercurial native. There is nothing too hot or too heavy for his ingenuity; nor is there anything too great for his fertile brain to accomplish. The United States, as a whole, are ruled by Gemini, the constellation of Mercury, and the restless energy, commercial enterprise, and scheming abilities, of the typical American are well expressed by the singular influence of his patron star.

Upon the Intellectual Plane, however, the planet Mercury is truly the genius of wisdom, and governs the whole of those mental qualities denominated perceptive. The oratorical powers are likewise ruled by this planet. Those dominated by its influx are ingenious, inventive, witty, sarcastic, scientific, and possess remarkable penetrative power. They are profound investigators of all those sciences that aid in the promotion of commerce.

Upon the Physical Plane, Mercury rules the brain and tongue. When strongly placed at birth, the person will possess a vivid imagination and retentive memory, and also be noted for mental capacity and power of persuasion.[57]

---

[57] Burgoyne continued (but Papus did not): "Such a position, if configured with the Moon, will give an unwearying fancy and strongly incline the mind towards the curious and Occult side of Nature. Should Mercury be ill dignified and void of the good aspects of other orbs, and at the same time be afflicted by Mars; he will produce a liar and an unprincipled, shuffling nature, incapable of attaining or appreciating the higher mental and moral standards. If strong or well aspected, and

The Moon

The symbolical aspect of Luna, like that of the Sun, cannot be detailed. From time immemorial the fair goddess of night has been venerated and worshipped as the universal mother; the feminine fructifying principle of all things. In the poetical conception of the Hebrews, the moon was called Ash-nem or Shenim, the state of slumber and change. Without a complete knowledge of astrological science, the weird truths concealed beneath the veil of Isis, can never be properly understood. Astrology alone, is the true key to the fundamental principles of Occultism. The secret of the tides; the mysteries of gestation; and the alternate periods of sterility and fruitfulness, caused by the ebb and flow of the magnetic life currents throughout every department of Nature; are discoverable only by a comprehension of the divine goddess of our midnight skies. This knowledge was the sublime attainment of the sages, "who," says Bulwer Lytton, "first discovered the starry truths that shone upon the great shemaia of the Chaldean lore." Chandra of the Hindoos; Isis of the Egyptians; Diana of the Greeks; and others, are all, the moon.

Kabbalistically, the Moon represents the soul of the grand man. It is, therefore, the celestial virgin of the world, in its mystical application; the emblem of Anima Mundi. Upon the esoteric planisphere, Luna becomes transformed into the Angel Gabriel. Upon the universal

---

below the horizon, he inclines the native to mystical and Occult studies; but if above the horizon and dignified, he confers a more external influence and produces orators, statesmen and teachers. One of the chief attributes of this planet, when well placed above the horizon, is that of literary ability. All such natives possess genuine talent in this direction. It may, therefore, be safely said that Mercury confers the ideal when below, and the practical when above, the ascendant at birth. Physically, Mercury gives a medium stature, strong but slender frame, exceedingly active, sharp piercing eyes, thin lips, well cut features and confident look. The complexion depends upon the Race."

Figure 16.   The Moon.

chart, we see her expressed as the divine Isis, the woman clothed with the sun. As Isis, she represents the grand initiatrix of the soul into the sublime mysteries of the spirit. The Moon, also, represents the molding, formative attributes of the astral light. She, also, stands as the representative of matter. Hence, in her dual character, she reveals to us her forces which are purely magnetic; and as such, they stand as the polar opposite of those of the Sun, which are electric. In their relation to each other, they are woman and man.

Astrologically considered, volumes might be written regarding this orb. When we consider her proximity to our earth, and her affinity with it, as well as the rapidity of her motion, we cannot help granting to her the highest position, as an active agent in every branch of judicial astrology. Her influence is purely negative, however; and in herself alone, or when void of the configurations of the Sun and planets; she is neither fortunate nor unfortunate. But, when configurated with other orbs; her influx becomes exceedingly potent as she receives and transmits to us the intensified influence of those stars aspecting her. The Moon, therefore, may be called the great astrological medium of the skies.

Upon the Intellectual Plane, Luna governs the physical senses, and to a great extent the animal passions also. She controls the lower forms of the domestic qualities, and the lower group of intellectual faculties. Those dominated by her influx are changeable in their nature, submissive and very inoffensive. Magnetically, their odylic sphere is purely mediumistic; hence, they become inactive and dreamy. Generally, Luna natives may be said to be rather indifferent characters, lacking anything and everything that may be called strong and decisive. They are given to roaming about, or constantly moving their residence from one place to another.

Upon the Physical Plane, the influence of the Moon is convertible in its nature, being harmonious or discordant according to her relative position to the sun and major planets.[58, 59]

---

[58] Burgoyne continued (although Papus did not): "If the Moon be dignified at birth; she renders the native more refined, engaging and courteous, than he otherwise would be. Should she also be well aspected; such a position will confer refined, artistic tastes, easy disposition, and good abilities. On the contrary, should the moon be ill dignified or evilly aspected, the native then born will be a shallow-minded, evil character, prone to dissipation, slothful, and void of proper business foresight, consequently, improvident. If the horoscope be a strong one in other respects, and points out sterling ability; then these aspects will tend rather towards making the person diplomatic. These aspects are also a strong indication, when unassisted by benevolent rays, of ultimate insanity. Very great consideration is necessary upon these conflicting points. In addition to the indifferent disposition above mentioned; the Moon, when rising, usually produces a medium-sized body, fair or pale complexion, round face and grey eyes; the forehead wide but not high; temperament phlegmatic."

[59] Burgoyne also gave full descriptions for Uranus and Neptune at this point, something Papus chose not to include. The other difference between the two treatments is that Papus followed the Chaldean order of the planets, shown here, whereas Burgoyne began with the Sun and Moon, and then discussed the planets in orbital order from Mercury to Neptune.

CHAPTER THREE

THE TWELVE SIGNS

FOR THE ASTRONOMER, AS we saw, the zodiac is merely the way of the mobile stars. Among the multiple constellations of the sky, the planets of our solar system have chosen twelve to constitute their path in the sky, and on this path they wander, more or less quickly according to their mass and their distance from the central Sun. (See figure 17 on page 48.)

The astrologer, on the contrary, in contrast to seeing simply masses of matter in these stars, discovers there a real physiology and in all of it a psychology. For the astrologer, the Earth is a living being, breathing, circulating and irritable. (See the works of Michel of Figanière.) Besides, the stars each have their representations on Earth. Some stones are a ray of a star fixed in matter. Some plants and some terrestrial animals are also "correspondents" of stars on the Earth. All ceremonial magic and also a great part of Hermeticism is based on acquaintance and the recall of these astral correspondences. Behold why astrology was so important to know well for all students of the ancient sciences.

When the Earth rotates in 24 hours, it produces one night and one day which, for the astronomer, is a simple physical phenomenon.

For the astrologer it presents each of the twelve signs of the zodiac[60] that could receive or send back different Spirits depending upon the sign which ascends at a city at a certain hour.[61]

For the hermetic philosopher, the Earth inhales the fluid of the Sun during the day and exhales it during the

---

[60] As a rising sign, or Ascendant.
[61] In other words, there is a different spiritual message, depending on which sign rises in a particular city at a particular time.

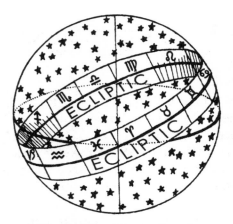

Figure 17.   The twelve signs.

night, accomplishing this breathing in 24 hours what humans accomplish twenty times in one minute.

In the same way, during its yearly movement around the Sun, the Earth sees one morning (Spring), one noon (Summer), one evening (Fall), and one night (Winter) parade around. This one day of the Earth symbolizes one year for terrestrial humans. And this day is consecrated to the circulation of the waters and to the fixing of the nervous fluid of the aforesaid Earth.

The notion of Time can therefore be interpreted differently according to one's point of view. One year of the gods corresponded previously to 365 terrestrial days.

If the stars are living beings, then what position do they occupy in the hierarchy of other beings? The problem was carefully studied by J.- J. Jacob, author of *The Sketch of all Universal Things,* and he established the hierarchy of living beings in the following manner: 1) Beings of Number; 2) Minerals; 3) the Force (or energy); 4) Plants; 5) Astral Beings; 6) Animals and Human Beings; 7) the Genies (Jinns). One will find the grounds for this classification in Jacob's books, as he was one of the masters of Hermeticism.

The place of the stars is characterized by the fact that a star doesn't move in concordance with another star. Plants don't move; animals, on the other hand, move at will. Figure 18 (page 50) summarizes this classification.

This concept that the star is a real being, with physiological organs, explains the spiritual and symbolic conceptions of esoteric astrologers. We understand the friends and the enemies of the planets, their predilection for one zodiacal sign, an astrological house, more than for one other house. We now go back to the zodiac.

We saw previously that the zodiac, the road of all the planets in the starry sky, is composed of twelve signs of which we studied the glyphs and the names. Every sign is divided by astronomers the same as for astrologers, into 30 degrees, the degrees in 60 minutes and the minutes into 60 seconds. It allows us to place each body very precisely in the zodiac.

For astrologers, the Sun seems to go up toward the North, and, when it reaches Cancer, who defines this North, it comes down again toward the equator up to Libra, then drives in through the signs of the winter and of misfortune. This march of the Sun was noted by the ancient observers, and most of the mythological narrations (like the Labors of Hercules) are based on this fact. Table 2 (page 51) indicates the character of each sign of the zodiac from the point of view of the obvious march of the Sun. On the 20th of March, the Sun returns to Aries, the first constellation, which was the point of departure.

The twelve signs are subdivided profitably in several different manners and it is indispensable, in order to study these subdivisions, to be able to recognize them in astrological works.

We first consider the four signs which indicate the cardinal points of the zodiacal sky; these are: to the East and to the vernal equinox, *Aries* (ascending) who begins the ascending signs of the zodiac. These ascending signs go from Aries to Libra, as we showed previously.

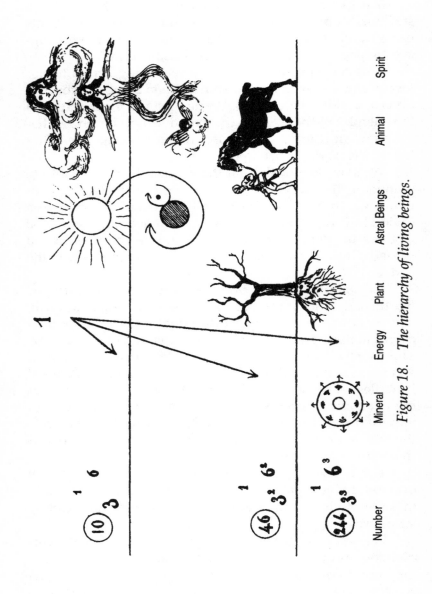

Figure 18. The hierarchy of living beings.

Table 2. The March of the Sun.

SEASON	SIGN	ADJUSTMENTS	MONTH
Spring	1 Aries	March forward (1st of the former year—the astrological New Year)	20 March – April 20
	2 Taurus	Squalls, anger (state of the atmosphere)	20 April – May 20
	3 Gemini	Calmness, sweetness of moderate temperatures (children of the air)	20 May – June 20
Summer	4 Cancer	First return to the Tropic of the Sun, bringing together noon at the horizon*	20 June – July 20
	5 Leo	Ardor of temperature and of heat	20 July – August 20
	6 Virgin	Crop times	20 August – 20 Sept
Fall	7 Libra	Equal days to the nights, equinox	20 Sept. – 20 Oct
	8 Scorpio	Times of dangerous illnesses	20 Oct. – 20 Nov
	9 Sagittarius	Times of hunting	20 Nov. – 20 Dec
Winter	10 Capricorn	New return or tropical of the Sun reapproaching noon at MC*	20 Dec. – 20 Jan
	11 Aquarius	Season of rains and some snows	20 Jan. – 20 Feb
	12 Pisces	Time of fishing prior to spawning	20 Feb. – March 20

* An odd expression to say the least. The point he was getting at is that Noon on the day of the Tropics (the solstices) in the temperate zone represents the time when the Sun stands closest to the true Zenith, the point perpendicular and pointing upward from the observer. Trans.

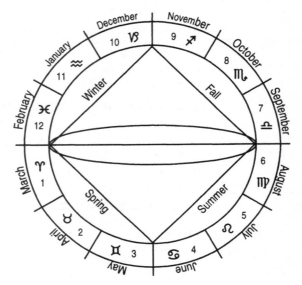

Figure 19.   The Great Celestial Cross.

To the North, at the winter solstice, is the northern angle of the zodiacal sky (Nadir), indicated by *Cancer*.

To the West, at the autumnal equinox, we see *Libra*, indicating the western angle. It is there that the descending signs of zodiac begins, and this goes from Libra to Aries.

Finally, to noon, or MC (Zenith) is *Capricorn*, mysterious door of celestial souls.

These four angular signs, *Aries, Cancer, Libra*, and *Capricorn* form the four points of the *Great Celestial Cross* of the equinoxes and solstices, origin of the symbolism of the cross in all its terrestrial adaptations.

Figure 19 will indicate these divisions clearly. Let us not forget that astrologers put the North at the base of their figures of the sky and noon at the highest point, whereas astronomers do the reverse.

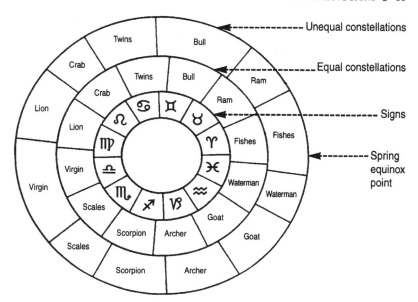

Figure 20. The differences between the tropical, sidereal, and
constellational zodiacs.

One understands that, if the Sun moves back every year
toward the South, in rising some degrees farther in a sign,
this rising determines a kind of time measurement, where
the Sun plays the role of the tip of the hand of a watch and
where the dial is represented by the zodiac as a whole, with
its twelve signs, constituting the hours of this immense
wheel of time. See figure 20.

The Sun takes, in round numbers, 2,000 years in order to
traverse each one of its hours, or every sign of the zodiac:
this makes 24,000 years (the exact numbers are: 2,147 years
by sign and 25,763 years for its tour of the zodiac) in order to
finish the twelve signs of zodiac. Every 24,000 years, there-

[62] i.e., as the constellation in which Spring begins shifts, there will be an overall
shift in the character of the Age.

fore, the Sun comes back to the point of the equinox where it was 24,000 years before. It is this number which constitutes the great year which has an influence in the march of the planetary constitutions[62] and in the production of deluges. The movement which produces this platonic year is called Precession of the Equinoxes, and it is characterized by this fact that the Sun arrives the following year to the equinox before the point where it was the previous year. The equinoctial point of a year precedes, therefore, the point of the previous year; from this comes the name Precession of the Equinoxes.

The Zodiac and the Astrological Houses

The signs of zodiac occupy a fixed location relative to each other in the sky. When a child is born in May, for example, how do astrologers operate in order to place the sign of the month in the East? In a very simple manner, they are going to use the astrological houses. Every sign of zodiac is going to constitute a house: Aries will be the 1st house, Taurus the 2nd house, and thus in succession up to 12th house for Pisces.*

Each of these houses is precisely like the corresponding sign with regard to the domiciles, exaltation, dignities, or falls of the planets.[63] The circle of astrological houses is inscribed on the circle of signs at the time of preparation of the horoscope, and the astrologer turns this circle of the houses to bring the house of the nativity to the Eastern cusp[64] whereas the signs preserve their place. So if one is born in May, the sign of Gemini will come to the East before the sign of Aries.[65]

The houses, like the signs, are Angular, Succedent, or Cadent,[66] and each presents a special temperament for the horoscope reading: the 1st house indicating the temperament of

---

* The zodiac and his adapted esoteric (*Mystéria*, Oct. 1913).
[63] Many astrologers would dispute this statement.
[64] In other words, the sign of the Ascendant is placed on the Eastern cusp.
[65] What Papus means is that at dawn, by definition, the sign ascending is the Sun sign for the month. Astrological dawn occurs when the Sun is conjunct the Ascendant.
[66] Equivalent to Cardinal, Fixed, and Mutable.

the Native (the person born at that time), the 2nd house, material interests, and thus in succession, as we will see later.

It is therefore very important to understand clearly the idea of the houses and of the zodiacal signs, and this conception is so much easier since there is complete similarity in the analogy between the two.

The whole sphere of the heavens is divided in two hemispheres by the horizon, and divided by the meridian in two halves, the Oriental or ascending, the other Western or descending, this gives four parts named quadrants, and every quadrant is then subdivided into three parts; one gets twelve divisions to which astrologers gave the name of houses of the horoscope.

These twelve houses serve as Significator, having connection to the whole life, as we will explain below.

Each one of these houses has a beginning and an end; the beginning is called a cusp and the end of this same house constitutes the cusp of the following house.

The twelve signs of the zodiac are found distributed on the twelve cusps of these houses, according to the hour and the latitude of the place of the birth of the child for whom one erects the horoscope. The characteristics of these twelve houses are listed below:[67]

In the 1st house one studies all that has connection to the conformation of the Native,[68] to his temperament, to his character, and to his faculties, good or bad.

The 2nd house informs us on all that touches the Native's pe-

---

[67] This set of descriptions of the houses is an unattributed paraphrase from Ély Star, *Les Mystères de l'Horoscope*, published in 1888. Star definitely had some variants in his house definitions compared to most other works, variants which form the basis of our identification of this section as being from his work. Incidently, this style of covering the same subject in several different ways in different places in the book is typical of French astrology books of this period.

[68] In French, the word for the Native is "consultant." Our English cognate would generally be understood to mean the astrologer, since the astrologer would be the consultant, and would refer to the Native as her/his client. However, the French usage reminds us of an interesting convention used by some astrologers, especially

cuniary interests: gains, profits of all natures, dealings, and transactions.[69]

The 3rd house studies the relative omens in regard to the short journeys,[70] to displacements, changes of places, as well as brothers,[71] to near relatives.

The 4th informs on parents (the father especially), and on possessions, and inheritances.[72]

The 5th is consulted for children [recreation],[73] and speculations.

The 6th informs on the family generally, on the underlings of all species, domestic; on the illnesses and struggles.[74]

---

those of a medical or horary persuasion. A chart is calculated for the time of the session. This chart is called the "consultation chart," and is used to delineate what the important themes will be in this particular consultation. In a medical context, the consultation chart shows the diagnosis and prognosis of the disease.

[69] Note: the selling of stocks and commodities are considered gambling by astrology, and are assigned to the 5th house. "Dealings" in this context is really closer to "commerce" or "profit-making" (hopefully) enterprise.

[70] The concept of short journeys astrologically in our era of air travel has become somewhat problematic. Short trips are assigned to the 3rd house, while long trips are assigned to the 9th. The translator suggests the following criteria. Characteristics of the 3rd-house journey: a place you have lived or visited before, one where you can feel comfortable maneuvering around, you have favorite restaurants, or places, you speak the language, and do not feel foreign there; 9th-house places are unfamiliar, awkward to get around in, where you are constantly reminded that you don't live there. Of course, there are people for whom the next suburb up the road is a 9th-house trip, and others for whom a trip halfway around the world may be to a place they have lived in before!

[71] And sisters.

[72] The specific associates of the 4th house with possession and inheritances are these: the 4th house rules buried treasure, and the inheritance of land, that which used to be called the patrimony. The latter term explains the specific association of the father with this house.

[73] This is evidently a mistake from Star's work: the word given for recreations was "emplois," which makes no sense in the context of the 5th house, since it means "employment," which is a 6th-house matter. Papus simply maintained Star's wording.

[74] This definition requires a bit of expansion. Papus' use of the 6th house for family is atypical and simply follows Star. The "underlings of all species" is really a

The 7th is the house of marriage: one discovers it also the declared enemies, quarrels, ruptures of association.[75]

The 8th gives the relative omens to unforeseen possessions [inheritances], to griefs of all sorts, and to the manner of death, natural or violent.

The 9th indicates the scientific faculties, long journeys, the ministry, religiosity and providential protections.

The 10th indicates the good or bad fortune of the Native, his social position, his elevation or his debasement.

The 11th is the house of friends, benefactors, associations, protections of all kinds.

The 12th indicates the tests whatever they are, inherent to all human life, slander, calumnies, hidden enemies, exiles and captivities.

The omens, good or bad, will depend on the influences of the planets that are placed in each one of these twelve houses, and made up by the signs of the zodiac for which here follows a survey, summarized, but sufficient. (See figure 21 on page 58.)

Aries symbolizes sacrifice. It is the symbol of our instincts. Natives born under this sign are intelligent, full of ardor, with an aggressive mind, energetic and imperious will. They are men of action, indomitable, refractory, despotic, petulant and quarrelers. They make excellent warriors.

---

reference to small or domesticated animals, where the dividing line between "small" and "large" is generally taken to be the sheep. "Illnesses" is self-evident, but "struggles" is not well illustrated in English sources, although Papus has an excellent pedigree, going back to Abraham Ibn Ezra's reference to the 6th house ruling "calumny."

[75] The association of the 7th house with quarreling is because of its mundane association with warfare and lawsuits.

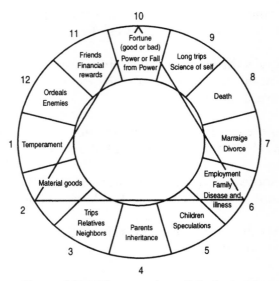

Figure 21. The meaning of the houses.

Taurus symbolizes fertility and procreative strengths. It gives a dull and reserved character, slow to become angry, then violent and furious, greedy, transported by the pleasures of the senses. It gives back, however, attentiveness, persistence. It rules industries and their various applications, as well as life-giving faculties and creative silent thought.

Gemini symbolizes the unit of action, the strength of union. It gives inspiration, energy in enterprises, a huge desire for learning, activity, a lot of imagination and of reason, a character a little lightweight and changing, but honest and generous. Following the eminent author of *The Light of Egypt*, this sign represents the union of reason and of intuition and, by following them, the most elevated state of incarnate humanity.

Cancer symbolizes the receding, the retrograde march. It must have contradiction and likes paradoxes. It influences the reflective powers in man and could make some mediums having direct inspiration. The people that are influenced by this sign are shy, liking to live retired; they are reflexive and sensitive. Their complexion is pale, delicate, feminine. Their conversation is pleasant and pleasing.

Leo is the symbol of strength and of courage. Leo dominates through the heart, gives great physical strength and powerful vital energy. Leo gives back generosity and niceness; makes for a powerful speaker, is impulsive, passionate, ardent and has an infectious will. Leo ideas always surpass the means of action. The mind is haughty, resolute, proud, ambitious.

Virgo symbolizes chastity. Subjects born under this sign are quiet, happy, satisfied, love study, instruction and, on the other hand, Virgo has a brain perfectly organized and gifted with intellectual superior capacities. Virgo gives hope and contentment with oneself, invites scientific applications, and gives a sanguine complexion and a petulant temperament.

Libra is the symbol of justice, measurement, distribution, equity. It gives interior perception, well balanced by intuition, providence, and reason. People born under this influence have ideas about fraternity and universal equality, but in theory only; they need to see personal benefit in order to put these ideas into practice. They rarely rise to elevated positions, by which they are too ponderous, too levelheaded and without great passionate movements. They command respect, and like the just middle in everything, they are excessive in nothing, and everywhere they are very close to the wisdom. This sign gives a fine complexion, a good agreeable and soft nature.

Scorpio symbolizes disappointments and death. They must excel in the ways of love, and this opens the door to abuse. It gives numerous ideas, crowds of projects and new conceptions, a sharp perception, a positive will. The natives excel as physicians, surgeons, chemists, and are capable in the mechanical arts. They are stout and strong, selfish, proud, and reserved.

Sagittarius is the symbol of the duality of nature. It gives a taste for sport, hunting especially. Natives under its influence have a certain worldly authority. It gives organized mind power, obedience and the faculty to command. The natives that it influences make prompt decisions; they have a big empire for themselves; they are beautiful of face, quick, energetic, skillful, faithful, generous, charitable and liking freedom. Their temperament is ardent, and their character benevolent.

Capricorn symbolizes sin. It is also the emblem of material servitude. Natives born under this sign are fertile in projects and always on the lookout for opportunities. They know how to discover in others all the weak points of which they will profit and benefit; hypocrites and beautiful talkers, they always promise and don't keep their promises. They don't like laborious works and don't know how to be energetic except when their interest is in the game. They are reserved and subtle, sometimes melancholic, selfish.

Aquarius is the symbol of trial. It represents the material phenomena and the intuitive or instinctive science, limited to that which is demonstrable to the senses. Natives influenced by the sign are robust, sanguine, elegant, agreeable, spiritual, distinguished.

Pisces is the symbol of the agitated stream; it gives a type of mental indifference, of nearly complete insouciance. The people born under this sign have pale complexions, some have fish eyes; they are shy, restful, capable of being influenced.

• • •

Like the planets, the signs of zodiac are classified into benefics and malefics. The Benefics are Taurus, Cancer, Leo, Virgo, Sagittarius and Pisces. The Malefics are Aries, Gemini, Libra, Scorpio, Capricorn and Aquarius.

They are, in addition, classified into four triplicities, each containing three signs corresponding to the four elements: Fire, Air, Earth, and Water.

> Signs of Fire: Aries, Leo, Sagittarius;
> Signs of Air: Gemini, Libra, Aquarius;
> Signs of Earth: Taurus, Virgo, Capricorn;
> Signs of Water: Cancer, Scorpio, Pisces.

In order to complete this brief survey of the twelve signs, we give below, in whole, the remarkable work of the author of *The Light of Egypt*, on the same topic.

We will next study the particular action of the zodiacal signs on the human body, their correspondences with the teachings of Polytheism, their divisions in sets of three signs: Triplicity, referring to the former division of the elements. We will finish in mentioning the masterly survey of the author of *The Light of Egypt* also, on the Triplicities.

Aries the Ram[76]

The sign Aries, in its Symbolical aspect, represents the Sacrifice. The flocks and herds bring forth their young during the portion of the year that the sun occupies this sign. In addition to the sacrifice, the Ram also symbolizes the spring and the commencement of a New Year, when life, light and love, are to be bestowed upon the sons of earth in consequence of the sun having once

---

[76] Rather than translate this extensive quotation from Thomas Burgoyne, I have inserted the text in the original English from *The Light of Egypt*, pages 239-252. Material quoted from *The Light of Egypt* has been set off in the text.

more gained the victory over the realms of winter and death. The symbol of the slain Lamb upon the equinoctial cross is another type of Aries.

Kabbalistically, the sign Aries represents the head and brains of the grand man of the cosmos. It is the acting, thinking principle in Nature called, sometimes, instinct, and again intelligence. Upon the esoteric planisphere, this sign is occupied by Benjamin, of whom Jacob, in his blessing to the twelve sons says 'Benjamin shall rave as a wolf, in the morning he shall devour the prey, and at night divide the spoils.' Above all other animals, the wolf is sacred to the planet Mars, and the sign Aries is under the special and peculiar control of this fiery planet. Mars is the most fiery of all the planets, and Aries is the first constellation of the fiery triplicity. The correspondence is significant. The Hebrews concealed this reference to the planetary nature of Mars by combining the wolf and the ram. 'The wolf in sheep's clothing' reveals to us the evil action of Mars when malefically posited in his own sign, the Ram. The Kabbalistical gem of this sign is the amethyst, and those born with Aries rising upon the ascendant of their horoscope, possess in this stone a powerful magnetic talisman. Aries is the first and highest emanation of the fiery triplicity, and is the constellation of the planet Mars.

Upon the Intellectual Plane, Aries signifies the martial spirit of destructiveness and aggression. It rules the head; 'Out of his mouth went a two edged sword.' It is the active will under the guidance of the executive forces of the brain; and those dominated by this influx[77] are imperious, dauntless, and energetic, in the first de-

---

[77] Remember that Burgoyne was writing this when the predominant model was that of the ether: thus, physical bodies as well as zodiacal signs emitted real rays or particles, which created their influence. Thus, the references to influx refer to this flow, in this case from the zodiacal sign.

gree. They will never really submit to the control of others.

Upon the Physical Plane,[78] Aries produces a spare but strong body, of medium height, long face, and bushy eye brows, rather long neck, powerful chest, complexion rather swarthy; disposition courageous, ambitious, intrepid, and despotic; the temper is fiery and passionate. Generally speaking, this sign gives a very quarrelsome, irritable, pugnacious person. Diseases are those of the head, small pox, measles, and fever. Of plants, this sign governs broom, holly, thistle, dock, fern, garlic, hemp, mustard, nettles, onions, poppies, radish, rhubarb and peppers. Of stones, Aries rules firestone, brimstone, ochre and all common red stones.

Taurus the Bull

The sign Taurus, in its Symbolical aspect, represents the powers of fecundity, and also the procreative forces in all departments of Nature. Its genius was symbolized as Aphrodite, who was generally represented as wearing the two horns upon her head in imitation of the Bull. Many mythologists have been deceived by this symbol, and have taken it to represent a figure of the crescent moon upon the head of Isis, whereas, it was the planet Venus which the ancients intended to symbolize, because she rules the constellation of the Bull by her sympathetic forces. Apis, the sacred Bull of the Egyptians, is another conception of Taurus. And as the sun passed through this sign during their plowing month, we also find this sign used as the symbol of husbandry.

---

[78] The references Burgoyne makes to the physical plane make the most sense when they are applied to the sign on the Ascendant, because it is the rising sign which is the strongest astrological influence on physical appearance.

Kabbalistically, this sign Taurus represents the ears, neck and throat of the grand old man of the skies, hence, this sign is the silent, patient, listening principle of humanity; also, it is the governor of the lymphatic system of the organism. Taurus, on the esoteric planisphere, is occupied by Issachar, which means hireling or servant. The patriarch, in his paternal blessing to Issachar, refers to the obedient, laborious nature of this sign, as follows: 'Issachar is a strong ass, crouching down between two burdens.' This is pre-eminently the earthy Taurine nature, as the ass and the ox are equally remarkable for their endurance as beasts of burden. The Kabbalistical gem of this sign is the agate, and therefore, this stone constitutes a natural talisman for those born with Taurus on their ascendant. Taurus is the highest emanation of the earthy trigon, and is the constellation of the planet Venus.

Upon the Intellectual Plane, Taurus signifies the quickening, germinating powers of silent thought and represents that which is pleasant and good, consequently, those dominated by this influx are able to choose and assimilate that which is good. They are slow to form opinions, are careful, plodding and self-reliant, and patiently await the realization of results. The chief mental characteristics are industry and application.

Upon the Physical Plane, Taurus gives a middle stature with strong, well-knit body, and short, thick, bull-like neck, broad forehead and dark hair, a dull complexion and rather large mouth. In disposition, the natives of the earthly trigon are sullen and reserved. They make firm friends, and unrelenting foes. Slow to anger, they are, like the bull, violent and furious when aroused. Of plants, this sign rules beets, plantain, coltsfoot, columbine, daisies, dandelions, gourds, myrtle, flax, larkspur, lilies, moss and spinach. Of stones, Taurus governs white coral, alabaster, and all common white stones that are opaque.

Gemini the Twins

The sign Gemini, in its Symbolical aspect, symbolizes unity, and the strength of united action, also the truths of matehood. The two bright stars, Castor and Pollux, represent the twin souls. The Greek myth of Castor and Pollux avenging the rape of Helen, is only a repetition of the biblical story of Simeon and Levi slaughtering the men of Shechem for the outrage committed upon their sister Dinah by the son of Hamor.

Kabbalistically, the sign Gemini represents the hands and arms of the grand man of the universe, and therefore, expresses the projecting and executive forces of humanity in all mechanical departments. Upon the esoteric planisphere, the sign is occupied by Simeon and Levi. 'They are brethren,' says Jacob, 'and instruments of cruelty are in their habitations,'—which refers in a very unmistakable manner to the fearfully potent powers of projection that lie concealed within the magnetic constitution of all those who are dominated by this sign. The mystical symbol of the twins conceals the doctrine of soul-mates and other important truths connected therewith. The mystical gem of this sign is the beryl, which means crystal, and consequently forms the talismanic stone for those born under the influence of this potential sign. Gemini is the first and highest emanation of the airy trigon, and is the constellation of the planet Mercury.

Upon the Intellectual Plane, Gemini signifies the union of reason with intuition, and those dominated by its influx express the highest mental state of embodied humanity. They are volatile, free, philosophical and generous. Their magnetic spheres are specially susceptible to the influence of inspirational currents. By nature they are restless and exceedingly energetic. They possess an excess of mental force which impels them headlong into the most gigantic enterprises. Their chief characteristics are intuitional and mental activity, consequently, they are nervous and restless.

Upon the Physical Plane, Gemini gives a tall, straight body, a sanguine complexion, dark hair, hazel or grey eyes, sharp sight and a quick, active walk. They possess a restless but gentlemanly appearance. In disposition, the natives of the airy trigon are volatile and fickle. They are scientific and possess a great passion for all kinds of knowledge: are inconstant, and rarely study one subject very long; are speculative, and possess large imaginations. Of plants, this sign rules privet, dog-grass, meadow-sweet, madder, woodbine, tansy, vervain and yarrow. Of stones, Gemini governs the garnet and all striped stones.

Cancer the Crab

The sign Cancer symbolizes tenacity to life. The crab, in order to move forward, is compelled to walk backwards; which illustrates the sun's apparent motion, when in this sign, where it commences to move backwards toward the equator again. It also represents the fruitful, sustaining essence of the life forces, hence, we see the symbol of the crab occupying a prominent position upon the breast of the statue of Isis, the universal mother and sustainer of all.

Kabbalistically, the sign Cancer signifies the vital organs of the grand man of the starry heavens, and therefore, represents the breathing and digestive functions of the human family, and also indicates the magnetic control of this constellation over the spiritual, ethereal and vital essences, and the capacity of those specially dominated by this nature to receive and assimilate the inspirational currents. Hence, Cancer governs the powers of inspiration and respiration of the grand man. The sign Cancer, upon the esoteric planisphere, is occupied by Zebulon, of whom his patriarchal father declares, 'Zebulon shall dwell at the haven of the sea, and he shall be for an haven of ships,' astrologically intimating the home of the crab, which is upon the sea shore. Its also expresses the varied powers of cohesion, and the paradoxical truths found in all contradictories. The mystical gem of the sign is the emerald. The stone constitutes a powerful talisman for all natives of Cancer, which is the highest emanation of the watery trigon, and is the constellation of the Moon.

Upon the Intellectual Plane, Cancer signifies the equilibrium of spiritual and material life forces. Those dominated by its influx express the highest form of the reflective powers; they are timid and retiring; are truly passive, and constitute natural mediums. Cancer possesses but little of the intuitional qualities. That which appears to be intuition is direct inspiration. To the external eye, the native of the watery trigon appear to be slothful; whereas they are incessant workers upon the higher or mental plane. This sign expresses to us the conservation of forces. Its chief attributes are sensitiveness and reflection.

Upon the Physical Plane, Cancer gives a medium stature, the upper part larger than the lower, a small, round face, pale or delicate complexion, brown hair and small, pensive grey eyes; disposition effeminate, timid and thoughtful; temper mild; conversation agreeable and pleasant. Of plants, this sign rules cucumbers, squashes, melons, and all water vegetation such as rushes, water lilies, etc. Of stones, Cancer governs chalk, selenite, and all soft, white stones.

Leo the Lion

The sign Leo symbolizes strength, courage and fire. The hottest portion of the year, in the northern hemisphere, is when the sun is passing through this sign. It is the solar Lion of the mysteries that ripens, with its own internal heat, the fruits brought forth from the earth by the moisture of Isis.

Kabbalistically, the sign Leo signifies the heart of the grand man, and represents the life center of the fluidic circulatory system of humanity. It is also the fire vortex of physical life. Hence, those born under this influx are noted for the superior strength of their physical constitution; and also for their wonderful recuperative powers after being exhausted by sickness. The sign Leo upon the esoteric planisphere, is occupied by Judah, of whom his dying parent says, 'Judah is a lion's whelp, from the prey my son thou are gone up. He stooped down, he crouched as a lion.' This sign reveals to us the mysteries of the ancient sacrifice, and the laws of compensation. The mystical gem of Leo is the ruby, and it forms a most potent disease-resisting talisman for all governed by the Leonine influx. Leo is the second emanation of the fiery triplicity, and is the constellation of the sun.

Upon the Intellectual Plane, Leo signifies the sympathies of the heart. Those dominated by its influx are generous even to excess with their friends. By nature they are deeply sympathetic, and possess that peculiar grade of magnetic force which enables them to arouse into action the latent sympathies in others. As orators their earnest, impulsive, pathetic style makes them an irresistible success. An exceedingly fine specimen of Leonine oratory is given in Genesis, chapter 44. This simple, eloquent appeal of Judah to Joseph, probably stands unequaled, for its sublime tenderness. The natives of Leo are impulsive and passionate, honest and faithful. Their mental forces are ever striving to attain unto some higher state; hence, their ideas are always in excess of their means to accomplish their large, majestic and grand plans.

Upon the Physical Plane, Leo gives a large, fair

stature, broad shoulders, large, prominent eyes, oval face, ruddy complexion and light hair, generally golden. This is for the first twenty degrees of the sign. The last ten degrees give the same but a much smaller person. Disposition high spirited, resolute, haughty, and ambitious. Of plants, this sign rules anise, camomile, cowslip, daffodil, dill, eglantine, eyebright, fennel, St. John's wort, lavender, yellow lily, poppy, marigold, garden mint, mistletoe, parsley and pimpernel. Of stones, Leo governs the hyacinth and chrysolite, and all soft yellow minerals such as ochre.

Virgo the Virgin

The sign Virgo symbolizes chastity, and forms the central idea of a great number of myths. The Sun-God is always born at midnight, on the 25th of December, at which time the constellation of Virgo is seen shining above the horizon in the east. Hence, originated the primitive idea of the Son of God, being born of a Virgin. When the sun passes through this sign the harvest is ready for the reaper; hence, Virgo is symbolized as the gleaning maid with two ears of wheat in her hand.

Kabbalistically, the sign Virgo signifies the solar plexus of the grand archetypal man, and therefore, represents the assimilating and distributing functions of the human organism. Consequently, we find that those born under this influence possess fine discriminating powers as to the choice of food best adapted to their particular organic requirements. This constellation, as governing the bowels of humanity, is highly important, since the intestines comprise a very vital section of the digestive organism and vital fluids. Upon the esoteric planisphere, Virgo is occupied by Asher. "Out of Asher, his bread shall be fat," says Jacob, "and he shall yield royal dainties." Thus typifying the riches of the harvest.

This sign expresses the fulfillment of the creative design, hence, the mysteries of maternity are concealed under this symbol. It also reveals to us the significance of the sacrament of the Lord's Supper. The mystical gem of Virgo is the jasper, a stone possessing very important virtues. It should be worn by all natives born under this sign. Virgo is the second emanation of the earthly trigon, and is the constellation of Mercury.

Upon the Intellectual Plane, the sign Virgo signifies the realization of hopes. Those dominated by this influx are calm, confident and contented; they are reflective and studious, and extremely fond of reading. Consequently, they become the mental repositories of much external wisdom and learning. Their chief attributes are hope and contentment. These desirable qualities, combined with the mental penetration of Mercury, which this sign contains, all conduce to make the native of Virgo pre-eminently fitted for the close application of scientific study. They possess large, well balanced brains and very superior intellectual abilities and make clever statesmen, when thrown into the vortex of political life.

Upon the Physical Plane, Virgo gives a medium stature, very neat and compact, dark sanguine complexion, and dark disposition; is ingenious, studious and inclined to be witty; rather even temper, but more excitable than Taurine persons. As orators, Virgo persons are fluent, plain, practical and very interesting. Of plants, this sign rules endive, millet, privet, succory, wood-bine, skullcap, valerian, wheat, barley, oats and rye. Of stones, the various kinds of flint.

Libra the Balance

This constellation, in its symbolical aspect, typifies justice. Most of our readers doubtless have seen the goddess of justice represented as a female, blindfolded, holding in her hand a pair of scales. This conception is purely astrological, and refers to the celestial Libra of the heavens. The sun enters this sign about the 21st of September, when, as the poet Manilius says:

Day and night are weighed in Libra's scales,
Equal awhile, at last the night prevails.

Kabbalistically, the sign Libra signifies the reins[79] and loins of the grand celestial man, and therefore, represents the central conservatory or store house of the reproductive fluids. It is also the magnetic vortex of procreative strength. This constellation also represents, in its most interior aspect, the equinoctial point of the arc in the ascending and descending cycle of the life atom. Therefore, this sign contains the unification of the cosmic forces as the grand central point of equilibrium of the sphere. Libra upon the esoteric planisphere, is occupied by Dan. The patriarch, in his blessing, thus refers to his celestial nature; 'Dan shall judge his people as one of the tribes of Israel.' Libra represents the interior equilibrium of Nature's forces, and contains the mystery of the divine at-one-ment of the ancient initiations. Upon the universal chart, this sign becomes Enoch, the perfect man. Its mystical gem is the diamond. As a magnetic talisman, this stone acts as a repulsive force, and combines with the magnetic sphere of those born under its influence, to repel the emanations from foreign bodies, either of persons or things. Libra is the second emanation of the airy triplicity, and is the constellation of Venus.

Upon the Intellectual Plane, Libra signifies external perception, balanced by intuition, the union of which

---

[79] That is, the kidneys.

72) ASTROLOGY FOR INITIATES

becomes externalized as reason and foresight. Therefore, those dominated by this influence constitute the rationalistic school of the world's body of thinkers. Theoretically, they are strong supporters of such conceptions as universal brotherhood, universal equality and the rights of man. But practically, they seldom (unless it pays) reduce their pet theories to actual practice. The natives of Libra, though possessing a finely balanced mental and magnetic organism, are seldom elevated into very prominent positions. This is because they are too even, both mentally and physically, to become the popular leaders of any radical or sensational party. It is one of the attributes of Libra, to infuse a natural instinct within all born under her influence to accept and adopt the golden mean, or, as it has been termed, 'the happy medium.' Hence, they generally command respect from both sides on questions of debate.

Upon the Physical Plane, Libra generally produces, when rising at birth, a tall, slender form, of perfect proportions, brown hair, blue sparkling eyes, and a fine clear complexion. The disposition is noble, amiable, high-minded and good. It is perhaps as well to note the fact that this sign often produces dark brown and black hair, and in females, very handsome features. Of plants, this sign rules watercress, white rose, strawberry, primrose, vines, violet, heartsease, balm, lemon, thyme and pansy. Of stones, Libra governs white marble, spar and all white quartz.

Scorpio the Scorpion

The sign Scorpio, in its symbolical aspect, symbolizes death and deceit. It is the allegorical serpent of matter mentioned in Genesis as tempting Eve. Hence, the so-called fall of man from Libra, the point of equilibrium, to degradation and death by the deceit of Scorpio. No wonder the primitive mind, when elaborating this sym-

bol, tried to express a spirit of retaliation; as Mackey
says, in speaking of these ancient races,

And as an act of vengeance on your part,
You placed within the sun a scorpion's heart

thus alluding to the brilliant star Antares.

Kabbalistically, the sign Scorpio typifies the generative organs of the grand man, and consequently, represents the sexual or procreative system of humanity. It
is the emblem of generation and life; therefore, the natives of Scorpio excel in the fruitfulness of the seminal
fluids, and this creates a corresponding increase of desire. A distinct reference to the fruitfulness of this sign
will be found in Genesis, chapter 30, wherein Leah,
when she beheld the birth of Zilpah's son, exclaimed, 'a
troop cometh' (see verses 10 and 11). Scorpio, upon the
esoteric planisphere, is occupied by Gad, of whom the
dying Jacob says, 'Gad, a troop shall overcome him,
but, he shall overcome at the last'; intimating the fall of
man from a state of innocence and purity, through the
multitude of sensual delights, and his final victory over
the realms of matter as a spiritual entity. This sign represents the physical plane of the attributes of procre-
ation. It contains the mystery of sex, and the secrets of
the phallic rites. The mystical gem of Scorpio is the
topaz, the natural talisman of those born under this influence. Scorpio is the second emanation of the watery
trigon, and is the constellation of Mars.

Upon the Intellectual Plane, the sign Scorpio signifies the generation of ideas; hence, those dominated by
this influx possess an inexhaustible resource of ideas and
suggestions. Their active evolutionary minds are ever
busy with some new conception, and their brains are literally crammed full of inventive imageries. They possess
keen perception, fine intuitional powers, and a very positive will. Hence, they excel as medical practitioners,

chemists and surgeons. In the various departments of the surgical art, natives of this sign possess no equal. In addition to this mechanical ability, they are endowed with a powerful, fruitful magnetic life force which they sympathetically transmit to their patients. This is why they become such successful physicians. The sexual desire is naturally very strong, hence, they are liable to excess in this direction.

Upon the Physical Plane, this sign gives a strong and rather corpulent body, medium stature, dark or ruddy complexion, dark hair, features often resembling the eagle; disposition active, resentful, proud, reserved, thoughtful and also selfish. Of plants, this sign rules blackthorn, charlock, heather, horehound, bean, bramble, leek, woad and wormwood. Of stones, lode stone, blood stone and vermillion.

Sagittarius the Archer

This constellation, in its Symbolical aspect, represents a dual nature, as it symbolizes retribution and also the hunting sports. We find it depicted as a Centaur, with the bow and arrow drawn to its head ready for shooting. Hence, it was frequently used to designate the autumnal sports, the chase, etc. The Centaur was also a symbol of authority and worldly wisdom. Mackey, speaking of this sign, said,

> The starry Centaur still bends the bow
> To show his sense of what you did below.

Kabbalistically, the sign Sagittarius signifies the thighs of the grand universal man. It, therefore, represents the muscular foundation of the seat of locomotion in humanity. It is the emblem of stability, foundation and physical power. This sign also represents the centers of physical, external, authority and command. Sagittarius, upon the esoteric planisphere, is occupied by Joseph. 'His bow abode in strength,' says the patriarch, 'and the arms of his hands were made strong.' It also represents the powers of 'Church and State,' and the necessity of legalized codes, civil, military and religious. It indicates to us the organizing powers of humanity, and the absolute necessity of 'the powers that be' in certain states of development. We see in Joseph the Egyptian ruler and law-giver, a true type of real authority. The mystical gem of this influx is the carbuncle, which is a talisman of great virtue to its proper natives. Sagittarius is the lowest emanation of the fiery trigon and is the constellation of Jove, the planet Jupiter.

Upon the Intellectual Plane, Sagittarius represents the organizing power of the mind; hence, this influence indicates the external powers of command, discipline and obedience, to the ruling authority of material institutions. Persons of this nature are loyal, patriotic, and law abiding. Such natives are generous and free; energetic and combative; hasty in temperament; ambitious of position and power; also charitable to the afflicted and oppressed. They possess strong conservative qualities; and their chief mental characteristics are prompt decision, self control, and the ability to command others.

Upon the Physical Plane, this sign usually produces a well formed person, rather above medium height, sanguine complexion, oval face, high forehead, bright brown hair, fine clear eyes; in short, handsome; in disposition, the native is quick, energetic, fond of out door sports and recreations; hasty tempered, jovial, free and benevolent. Of plants, this sign rules agrimony, wood betony, feather-few[80] and mallows. Of stones,

---

[80] A less common name for feverfew. The attribution here is slightly atypical. Blagrave, Ramesey and Dariot gave feverfew to Jupiter, hence, Sagittarius, as one of the signs of Jupiter, could be used. However, Culpeper gave feverfew to the Sun and Venus, and Gadbury concurred on Venus.

Sagittarius governs the turquoise, and all the stones mixed with red and green.

Capricorn the Goat

This sign, in its symbolical aspect, typifies sin. The scapegoat of the Israelites; and the universal offering of a kid or young goat as an atoning sacrifice for sin, are significant. The different qualities of the sheep and goat, from a symbolical standpoint, are used by St. John in his mystical Apocalypse. The Redeemer of mankind, or Sun God, is always born at midnight directly Sol enters this sign, which is the winter solstice, 'The young child' is born in the stable and laid in the manger of the goat, in order that he may conquer the remaining signs of winter or death, and thus save mankind from destruction.

Kabbalistically, the sign Capricorn signifies the knees of the grand macrocosm and represents the first principle in the trinity of locomotion, viz., the joints: bending, pliable and movable. It is the emblem of material servitude and as such is worthy of notice. Capricorn, upon the esoteric planisphere, is occupied by Naphtali, whom Jacob says, 'is a hind let loose, he giveth goodly words.' Here we have two very distinct references; the first, to the symbol, a hind or young deer, i.e., a goat with horns (goats and deer are equally significant of the earthly, mountainous nature, and are fond of high hills); the second is the Christmas proclamation, he giveth goodly words, 'Peace on earth, good will towards man.' This sign represents 'regeneration,' or rebirth, and reveals the necessity of 'new dispensations.' The mystical gem of this constellation is the onyx, sometimes called 'chalcedony.' Capricorn is the lowest emanation of the earthy trigon, and is the constellation of the planet Saturn.

Upon the Intellectual Plane, Capricorn signifies external form, and those dominated by its influx are among the very lowest in the scale of true spirituality. The brain of this influence is ever on the alert to seize and take advantage if circumstances. The sign gives a purely scheming mentality; the intellectual nature is directed purely to the attainment of selfish ends; the penetrating power of the mind is great. The natives are quick as lightening to see in others the weak points that they may work to their own advantage. They are indisposed to do any real hard work unless they see some great benefit therefrom in the immediate future. It is a very undesirable influence.

Upon the Physical Plane, Capricorn generally gives a medium stature, slender, often ill proportioned; plain looking, energetic in their own interests, and indolent in the employ of others. Frequently these natives have a long sharp chin and slender nose, with small piercing eyes. They are almost always narrow chested. In disposition, they are crafty, subtle, reserved and often melancholy. At the same time, native of Saturn are often miserly. Of plants, this sign rules hemlock, henbane, deadly nightshade and black poppy.[81] Of stones, Capricorn governs coal and all black or ash colored minerals.

Aquarius the Water Bearer

This sign symbolizes judgment. This constellation forms the starry original of the urn of Minos, from which flow wrath and condemnation or blessings and reward, according to the works done in the body, irrespective of theological faith. The earlier baptismal urns of the primitive Christians, and the elaborate stone

---

[81] Are all Capricorn-ruled plants poisonous or inedible? No, but not far from it! Capricorn also rules African amaryllis and comfrey.

fonts of the later churches, are relics of this great astral religion.

Kabbalistically, the sign Aquarius signifies the legs of the grand archetypal man, and therefore, represents the locomotive functions of the human organism. It is the natural emblem of the changeable, movable and migratory forces of the body. The Water-bearer, upon the esoteric planisphere, is occupied by Reuben. 'The excellency of dignity and the excellency of power,' says Jacob, 'unstable as water thou shalt not excel.' A simple but magnificent astrological description of this sign, which, from time immemorial, has been symbolized by two wavy lines, like the ripples of running water. This sign signifies consecration, and not only contains the rites and mysteries of consecration, but will reveal to the student the potency of all sacred and dedicated works. The mystical gem of this sign is the sky blue sapphire (not the dark or opaque sapphire). Aquarius is the lowest emanation of the airy trigon, and the constellation of Uranus.[82]

Upon the Intellectual Plane, Aquarius represents popular science, and consequently, the truth of material phenomena. Those dominated by its influx constitute the school of inductive philosophy; the grand basis of all esoteric science. They represent the intellectual and scientific spirit of their age and generation; and cannot advance one step beyond these classes of facts which are demonstrable to the senses. Elegant in form, they are brilliant in intellect.

---

[82] Papus did not appear to use the so-called modern rulerships of the signs (Uranus for Aquarius, Neptune for Pisces, and now Pluto for Scorpio), but here Burgoyne applies them. One concept is completely absent from Burgoyne's descriptions of the signs, namely whether the sign is Cardinal, Fixed or Mutable. Cardinal signs are good at starting things, but not so good at follow-up; Fixed signs are stubbornly attached to the status quo; Mutable or common signs shift with the wind. This is especially relevant here, because Aquarius is a fixed sign. Thus, to apply such words as "changeable," "moveable," or "unstable" are a considerable strain to a typical description of the sign.

Upon the Physical Plane, Aquarius gives a medium stature, plump, well-set and robust; good, clear, sanguine complexion; sandy or dark flaxen hair; very prepossessing appearance; disposition elegant, amiable, good natured, witty and very artistic; fond of refined society. Of plants, this sign rules spikenard, frankincense and myrrh. Of stones, Aquarius governs black pearl and obsidian.

Pisces the Fishes

This sign symbolizes the flood; chiefly because, when Sol passes through this sign the rainy season commences; clearing away the snows of winter, the melting torrents of which flood the valleys and lowlands.[83] This sign is also the terminus of Apollo's journey through the twelve signs.

Near their loved waves cold Pisces keep their seat,
With Aries join, and make the round complete.

Kabbalistically, the sign Pisces signifies the feet of the grand cosmic man; and therefore, represents the basis or foundation of all external things as well as the mechanical forces of humanity. It is the natural emblem of patient servitude and obedience. This sign, upon the esoteric planisphere is occupied by Ephraim and Manasseh, the two sons of Joseph, who received their portion in Israel as the two feet of the grand, archetypal man. It signifies confirmation, also baptism by water. It also indicates to us the divine purpose of the great cycle of necessity; commencing with the disruptive, flashing,

---

[83] An interesting description, given that Western astrology as we know it developed in the Fertile Crescent at about 30–35° North Latitude. Not exactly descriptive of the climate of the Middle East, much less Egypt or the Mediterranean!

dominating fire of Aries, and terminating with its polar opposite, water, the symbol of universal equilibrium. The mystical gem of Pisces is the chrysolite (white and glittering). Pisces is the last emanation of the watery trigon, and is the constellation of Neptune.

Upon the Intellectual Plane, Pisces represents mental indifference. It is the polar opposite of the head. Those dominated by its influx express a peculiar indifference to those things which generally interest others. They take all things as they come, and pay no serious attention to any. They live and die in accordance with St. Paul's advice, being 'all things to all men.'

Upon the Physical Plane, this sign gives a short, fleshy body, brown hair, pale complexion, moist, watery eyes (fishy looking); disposition negative, timid, listless and harmless. Their nature is peaceable, but their actions are influenced by their surroundings and friends. Of plants, this sign rules all sea weeds, also ferns and mosses that grow in water. Of stones, it governs coral, rock, pumice and gravel or sand.

Let's now consider our connections to the zodiacal signs (see figure 22 on page 81). There are first the stationary connections, those that don't vary. In this category, we will signal the connections of the signs of zodiac and of physical body of the human being.

Aries corresponds to the head, Taurus to the shoulders, and thus in succession, according to the following figure through to the feet, to which corresponds the [sign] of Pisces.

To serve this correspondence, the following means is the simplest. The sign which dominates the birth indicates the part of physical body the most subject to troubles. So a person born between 21 March to April 20, is under the sign of Aries, and is subject to troubles of the head and to the accidents involving the head. A person born under the sign of Pisces is subject to accidents involving the feet.

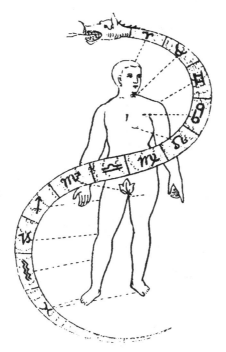

Figure 22. The zodiac and the physical body.

In order to create an idea of the significance of the signs of the zodiac, we must study them separately, recalling that the revolution of the Earth brings successively all the twelve signs into influences over our everyday existence. Table 3 shows the signs as we know them. (See page 82.)

The seven major planetary geniuses govern the head, seat of the intelligence and of the will: *Rempha,* genius of *Saturn,* governed the left eye. *Pi-Zeus,* genius of *Jupiter,* governed the right eye. *Ertosi,* genius of *Mars,* governed the right nostril. *Pi-re,* genius of the *Sun,* governed the forehead. *Suroth,* genius of *Venus,* governed the left nostril. *Pi-Hermes,* genius of *Mercury,* governed language. *Pi-joh,* genius of the *Moon,* governed the brain.

Table 3.   Mystery of the Twelve Signs of the Zodiac.

I.   *Amun*, genius of *Aries*, governed the head and its illnesses.

II.   *Apis*, genius of *Taurus*, governed the collar, the shoulders and their illnesses.

III.   *Hercules-Apollo*, genius of *Gemini*, governed the arms, the hands and their illnesses.

IV.   *Hermanubis*, genius of *Cancer*, governed the chest, the lungs, the ribs, the spleen and their illnesses.

V.   *Momphtha*, genius of *Leo*, governed the stomach, the heart, the liver and their illnesses.

VI.   *Isis*, genius of *Virgo*, governed the spleen, the stomach, the intestines and their illnesses.

VII. *Omphtha*, genius of *Libra*, governed the dorsal spine, the loins and their illnesses.

VIII.   *Typhone*, genius of *Scorpio*, governed the hips, the sexual organs and their illnesses.

IX.   *Nephte*, genius of *Sagittarius*, governed the thighs and their illnesses.

X.   *Anubis*, genius of *Capricorn*, governed the knees and their illnesses.

XI.   *Canopis*, genius of *Aquarius*, governed the legs and their illnesses.

XII. *Ichthon*, genius of *Pisces*, governed the feet and their illnesses.

To the polytheistic Greco-Romans, the 12 major gods corresponded to the 12 signs of the zodiac, in the following [order]: *Minerva* to *Aries; Venus* to *Taurus; Apollo* to *Gemini; Mercury* to *Cancer; Jupiter* and *Cybele* to *Leo; Ceres* to *Virgo; Vulcan* to *Libra; Mars* to *Scorpio; Diana* to *Sagittarius; Vesta* to *Capricorn; Juno* to *Aquarius; Neptune* to *Pisces.*

In the Hebrew Kabbalah, the twelve tribes of Israel, and the twelve precious stones which decorated the breastplate of the High Priest, corresponded to the signs of zodiac, in the following order: the tribe of Gad and the amethyst to *Aries*; the tribe of Ephraim and the hyacinth to *Taurus*; the tribe of Manassah and the chrysoprase to *Gemini*; the tribe of Issachar and the topaz to *Cancer*; the tribe of Judah and the beryl to *Leo*; the tribe of Naphthali and the chrysolite to *Virgo*; the tribe of Asher and sardonix to *Libra*; the tribe of Dan and sardonix to *Scorpio*; the tribe of Benjamin and emerald to *Sagittarius*; the tribe of Zebulon and chalcedony to *Capricorn*; the tribe of Reuben and the sapphire to *Aquarius*; the tribe of Simeon and jasper to *Pisces.*[84]

Let us pass on to a survey of the triplicities.

---

[84] This list is *extremely* problematic. First, there is no agreement on the attribution of the Twelve Tribes to particular zodiacal signs. An alternate listing is: Gad = Virgo, Ephraim = Libra, Manassah = Scorpio, Issacher = Taurus, Judah = Aries, Naphthali = Aquarius, Asher = Pisces, Dan = Capricorn, Benjamin = Sagittarius, Zebulon = Gemini, Reuben = Cancer, and Simeon = Leo. Even Burgoyne gives a different listing on page 236: Benjamin = Aries, Issacher = Taurus, Simeon = Gemini, Zebulon = Cancer, Judah = Leo, Virgo = Asher, Libra = Gad, Sagittarius = Joseph, Capricorn = Naphthali, Aquarius = Reuben, and Pisces = Ephraim and Manassah. The second problem is that the breastplate of the High Priest between the First and Second Temple differed in the stones used. The third problem is that stones have made it to this list which are not found in the Middle East, nor have they ever been found in artifacts taken from Egypt or the Middle East. This means that they were neither mined nor traded, thus it is difficult to imagine how they could have been original citations from ancient works, and not later attributions. Chrysoprase is a stone which falls in this category. The fourth problem is one specific to this text: the word that Papus used for the stone for Libra was *sardoine*, while that for Scorpio was *sardonix*. These words are synonyms of each other! It is quite possible that Papus did not know this, but simply used the words given in his immediate source, or this was a typographical error.

The Triplicities of the Signs

The ancients attached a very great importance to the division of the signs in four series, each one of three signs, and referred to this ancient division as the elements: Fire, Water, Air, and Earth.

The ancients taught that the sky had a dominant action on physical forces, living beings and the states of the matter on the Earth. That is how they gave the name of Earth to all this which was in the solid state, the name of Water to all this which was in the liquid state, the name of Air to all this which was in the gaseous state, and the name of Fire to all the demonstrations of Force. It is a gross mistake to believe that these terms designated the Earth, itself, or terrestrial Water, or the atmospheric Air, or the Fire of a furnace; the use of such metaphorical expressions as antimony for Earth, Eau-de-Vie (brandy), Air (or Spirit) of Wine, philosophical Fire, etc., etc., would serve the need to illuminate the concept to the profane.

These various states of matter were indicated symbolically by triangles: Fire, by a triangle the tip pointed upward but not blocked to its top; air by a triangle the point upward and blocked at its top; Water, by a triangle the tip pointed downward and not blocked; Earth, by a triangle pointed downward, blocked at its top.

You can now understand what this adept, the author of *The Light of Egypt*, has to say on the topic of triplicity.[85]

> The four triplicities symbolize the four cardinal points of the universe. To us, on our present external and internal plane, they signify the four opposite points of space as represented in the compass and cross (hence the sacredness of the cross as a symbol in all times and

---

[85] Rather than translate this extensive quotation from Thomas Burgoyne, we have quoted the original English, pages 252–255. Quoted material has been set off in the text.

ages) and the four Occult elements: Fire, Earth, Air and Water. They each correspond to a particular quarter of the heavens. Thus, the Fiery Trigon corresponds to the positive-azoth; and is expressed in the glowing, flaming, eastern horizon at sunrise; the beginning of the day. Similarly, primary molten fire was the beginning, or first condition, of the present order of things on our globe; and stands for that principle of heat termed caloric, which sustains the animal, vital force of all animate beings upon the face of the planets.

Upon the Intellectual Plane, Fire represents zeal, animal courage, daring; and in fact, all that pertains to action and activity. While on the higher (esoteric) plane, Fire implies the interior apprehension of the meaning and significance of actions as displayed in the trinity, and expressed by fire of three terms as Aries, Leo, and Sagittarius; Aries the intellect; Leo the emotions; Sagittarius the offspring of the intellect and emotions; the external result or consummation of the two; that point which is neither the one nor the other; but where the two are one.

The Earthly Triplicity stands for the frozen, inert north, as a symbol of rigidness, hardening, crystallization, death. It is concerned with all phenomena that is the most external and palpable to the external senses; the solids, metals, fabrics.

Upon the Intellectual Plane, it is concerned with the relations of solids to each other, from which is especially evolved form, proportion, sound, etc. The same may be said of the metals dug up from the bowels of the earth, of the commerce, arts and industries resulting therefrom. Esoterically, the earthy trigon denotes the comprehension of the spiritual qualities evolved from the earthly activities; or, rather, that one spiritual quality of three-fold formation expressed in three mystical terms; Taurus, servitude or spirit of patient work; Virgo, formation and re-formation; Capricorn, the result of the union of Taurus and Virgo, which leads either to the higher plane in the spiral of existence, or to the lower plane on the downward course to the darker realms of being; more earthy, hardened and dead.

The Airy Triplicity represents the west; the scene of the setting sun; which signifies the dying of the day, of sense and of matter; which is only the promise of another day; an advance to a higher plane. This brighter day is denoted by the airy trigon; and is concerned, upon the external plane, with the priestly, political and social relations of human life. That is to say, it represents the higher qualities of these relations. It is, therefore, symbolized by the invisible element, air; the great medium of motion. Its esoteric significance is comprised in the arcana of the one true science. After first having a knowledge of the twins (Gemini) external, the internal science attains unto the adjustment or equilibrium or balance (Libra) of the two; so that they exactly blend in the divine equipoise of harmony and wisdom; thus realizing only the rippling waves (Aquarius) of peaceful results; instead of the downpouring floods and cataclysms; both social and physical; which otherwise result from the unbalanced scales (Libra); when external and internal antagonize, as two hostile and absolutely separate and dual forces; instead of balancing as two modes of one and the same eternal motion, the one life of the universe.

The Watery Triplicity, symbolical of the south, is the exact opposite of the earthy north. It is the frozen, melted; the hardened, liquified; the renewal of the crystal into the other forms; and the resurrection of death into life. The watery trigon signifies the constant effort in Nature to adjust opposites and contradictions; to bring about chemical changes and affinities as especially seen in fluids; and as so perfectly symbolized in that great distinguishing feature of water, viz., to seek its own level. On the external plane of human life, the watery trigon denotes love; sex (Scorpio and Mars); the offspring (Pisces); the external results of the union of the two (love and sex). On the more esoteric planes, Cancer symbolizes the tenacity of life, hence, the desire for immortality; which, combined with a knowledge of the mysteries of sex (Scorpio and Mars) or generation and regeneration, lead the immortal soul to the termination of its earthly pilgrimage and material incarnations, in the union with its missing half or Pisces, which is symbolized, upon the celestial equator (equilibrium), as the two fishes bound together by the cord (of love). Having regained the equator and passed from the lower arc of matter, the soul enters once more upon the spiritual path of eternal conscious life.

The reader will now perceive that the four great trigons are but the different series of attributes within the human soul or microcosm; and further, that the twelve constellations of the zodiac reveal the mystical signification of Adam Kadmon,[86] the archetypal man of the starry planisphere. Thus, Aries rules the head, brain and the fiery will; Taurus the neck and throat, the ears, the listening requisites of obedient servitude; Gemini the hands and arms, or projective and executive powers; Cancer the breast, bosom and lungs, which signify life and love; Leo the heart and its varied emotions; Virgo the bowels, the navel or maternal, the compassionate and formulative qualities; Libra the loins or physical strength, the power of balancing the mental faculties; Scorpio the generative organs and the procreative attributes; Sagittarius the hips and thighs, the seat or foundation of volitional force, the migratory instincts; Capricorn the knees, tokens of humble submission to the higher powers; Aquarius the legs and ankles or active powers of movement and locomotion; and

---

[86] The archetypal Adam, the first man.

lastly, Pisces the feet, the foundation of the whole frame, which should ever be capable of finding and sustaining its own level unaided, lest the grand human temple fall to the ground. Thus we begin with fire and terminate with water. These constitute the two poles of the human magnet.

NOTE: To obtain the celestial application of the above, the points must be reversed; north becomes south; east becomes west, and so on.

CHAPTER FOUR

APPLICATIONS OF ASTROLOGY

ASTROLOGY IS THE KEY to any good result from the application of occult sciences. These applications ensue logically from the reality of astral influences on nature and on humans. These influences, once admitted—and the experimental method will soon convince all serious researchers—will allow us to easily understand all the parts that we are capable of pulling together.

Our goal was not to write a didactic treatise of astrology, or merely to awaken attention, but to insist on the importance of these studies. We will now mark off some details on the application of astral influences to magic, to medicine, and to the divinatory sciences. We will refer the reader to more complete works for the survey of the larger question upon which astrology could shed some real light: birth, heredity, criminality, education, etc., and we recommend to the reader the works of Haatan, Selva, Flambart, etc.[87]

Applications in Magic

Knowledge of the signs of the zodiac and of their action, knowledge of the planets and of their properties and correspondences are absolutely indispensable to the magician under pain of complete failure in all his works. We will, however, reduce the exposition of necessary principles to strict necessity, and will reject in this exposition all the conventional teachings that don't correspond to a natural reality.

---

[87] All the works cited are generally out of print. However, for our purposes, the mention of Henri Selva is significant, because Selva's work was the return of the method of Morinus to astrology. In that regard, as cited in my Introduction, the works of Weiss are especially significant.

The Signs of the Zodiac

The signs of zodiac are twelve in number. Their numeration begins at Aries, which corresponds to the month of March, and each one of them takes care of 30° on the celestial sphere. Like, in the *Connaissance des Temps*,[88] one finds the position of the stars indicated in degrees, it is important to well recall the positions of the signs of the zodiac with regard to the celestial sphere. The positions are the following:

March	Aries	0 to 30°
April	Taurus	30 to 60°
May	Gemini	60 to 90°
June	Cancer	90 to 120°
July	Leo	120 to 150°
August	Virgo	150 to 180°
September	Libra	180 to 210°
October	Scorpio	210 to 240°
November	Sagittarius	240 to 270°
December	Capricorn	270 to 300°
January	Aquarius	300 to 330°
February	Pisces	330 to 360°

The seven planets that magic considers as the sole useful ones, not taking into account any others,[89] are, in the order adopted by magic:

Saturn
Jupiter
Mars
Sun

---

[88] A contemporary work. The important point was not the work itself, but the idea that the signs, as shown in the following table, can be expressed in a 360° notation as well as degrees of a sign. This is especially useful to such operations as the calculation of Arabic parts.

[89] i.e., Uranus, Neptune, and now Pluto.

Venus
Mercury
Moon

We know that this classification is based on appearances and in taking the Earth as the center of the solar system. Astronomically, the order of the stars is, as our reader knows, the following: [Pluto], (Neptune, Uranus) Saturn, Jupiter, Mars, Earth and Moon, Venus, Mercury, the Sun; they take as the point of departure the real center of system: the Sun.

The seven stars turn in the sky the way that the hands of a watch turn around the dial. But the celestial clock would have, in the teaching of the hermeticians, seven gifted hands of more or less rapid movements.

The stars are, for most people and circumstances, intelligent centers broadcasting astral power; this can be of prime importance in making an idea possible in certain respects. We won't go into progressively more technical detail, in part to avoid as much as possible the inherent obscurity involved in these sorts of questions. Let's first examine the stars individually, without concerning ourselves with their connections with one another or with the celestial houses; and let us begin with our own satellite.

The Moon

The Moon particularly dominates this so-called physical world on Earth, the one called the sublunar realm in Hermeticism. This satellite, which is nearly negligible if we consider our solar system as a whole, acquires, however, an exceptional importance for the inhabitant of the Earth, for the practical magician an importance equal to the Sun, such that in a pinch it is sufficient to guide oneself solely on these two stars in order to succeed, or to assure an advantage, in all operations undertaken.

The Moon is the astral matrix of all terrestrial productions for which the Sun is the living father. We already spoke of the remaining action of planetary moons as being like

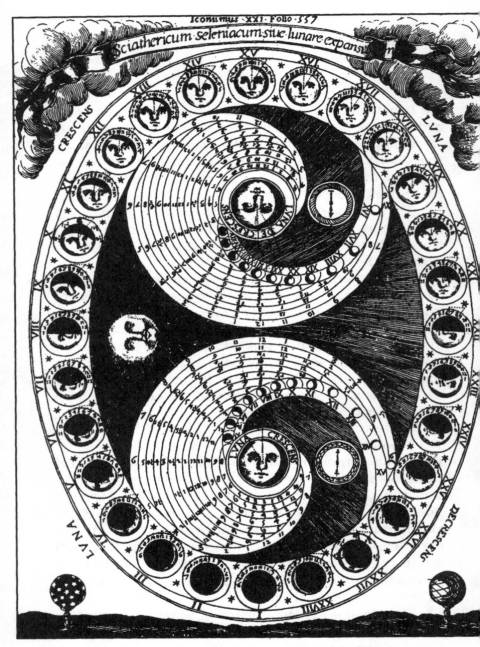

Figure 23. *The lunar cycle of 28 days (after Kircher).*

nervous ganglia for the their own planets. Everything which comes to the Earth, emanations and souls, passes by the Moon and all this which is part of the Earth passes it also.[90]

The Moon reproduces analogously, in its phases, the universal law of involution and of evolution in four periods. During the first part of its course (New Moon to Full Moon) the Moon behaves according to appearances. It is the only moment that must be used by the magician for operations involving illumination; it is also the moment when the lunar influences are really dynamic.

Speaking of which, permit us to add parenthetically: a rich industrialist, with joie-de-vivre, and mocking "prejudices" that he encountered, was once exploiting woodland in the Jura. Seeing that his competitors carefully restricted themselves to cutting the trees during the decreasing period of the Moon (Full to New), he laughed a lot at their superstition and benefitted from inexpensive manpower during the increasing period in order to exploit his fortune extensively. Two years later, our industrialist had become more superstitious than the others, because all the cuttings made during this period of the lunar cycle could hardly wait to rot. "One doesn't know why," said he, but it was because of him that we know this story.

So the ascending phase of the Moon has very great importance according to the teachings of magic. We will soon return more extensively to this luminary by the way of the lunar mansions. The color corresponding to the Moon is white.

Mercury

The fastest of the planets and the one nearest the Sun, Mercury represents childhood with its excess of vitality and

---

[90] This is yet another reference to the Medieval idea of the sublunar world. As the celestial sphere closest to the Earth, the lunar sphere was the mediator, so to speak, for all the astral or spiritual energy coming to the Earth, and then also leaving the Earth.

movement. It accomplishes its (revolutionary) cycle in 88 days. This permits those who use its influence from the magical point of view to do so at least four times a year. The color corresponding to Mercury is the entire spectrum; that is to say, the juxtaposition of different colors; this indicates the tendency to change, which one does well to assign to all that depends on Mercury. In ancient grimoires, one wrote the name of this planet with a different color for each one of the letters comprising its name.

Venus

The star of morning.—the feminine youth with all its co-quetteries, its seductions, and its dangers, the Goddess of Love in all its modes reigns over the lover, whereas the chaste Diana, the Moon, reigns over the mother. The cycle of Venus is accomplished in 224 days and 16 hours. Those who place a great deal of importance on operations done under the influence of this planet, because of a missed date, are delayed nearly a year for the return of a favorable moment. Venus is in rapport with the color green.

The Sun

The boiling Apollo—youth with its generosities, noble ambitions and pride, and also foolhardiness and inexperience in practical things; art with divine intuition, horror and disdain of the vulgar. The Sun is the father, the universal generator of our world; also its influences in magic is considerable. This influence is calculated according to the position taken by the Day Star with regard to the zodiacal signs. The feasts of Christianity—Christmas, Easter, St. John—are solar festivals, as we will have the opportunity to observe shortly. The color corresponding to the Sun is golden yellow.

Mars

The planet nearest to Earth—reddish and violent, Mars is the picture of the man of war. Mars possesses courage, energy, anger and violence. The influence of Mars is used to put magic into action. But the cycle of this planet being 687 days, nearly two times the terrestrial year, doesn't bode well often for influential direction of Mars for the preparation of pantacles.[91] One uses either the planetary days or the consecrated[92] hours, as the analogous connections to the Moon in the signs. The red of fire corresponds to the color of Mars.

Jupiter

The man of reason and will in whom the violence and angers of youth are alleviated, and who is a veritable master of himself: such is the aspect that Jupiter shows to us. Quiet and methodical, Jupiter is twelve times slower than Earth, taking 11 years, 10 months, and 17 days precisely to accomplish his cycle. It is true that the bracing influence of the Sun disappears more quickly than on our planet, the day being half as long as on Earth.[93] In magic, the influence of Jupiter gives honors and glory, and can therefore be used only in exceptional cases. The color of Jupiter is metallic blue.

Saturn

The old man, the sad man, but long on experience, takes nearly 30 years (29 years and 187 days) to accomplish its complete cycle and deal out long but somber life to all those who are born under its influence. Saturn is the beloved star of black magicians, who love the decreasing Moon as well. The color of Saturn is leaden or metallic black.

Such is the first idea that one can form about the living stars of our system. As we see it, Mercury, the Sun, Mars, Jupiter,

---

[91] Pantacles are emission fluids, used for their magical action as universal essences. Their action was considered as a kind of amulet: a passive defense against "influences," compared to the more active approach of talismans.
[92] Planetary.
[93] Amazing, isn't it, that a body so much bigger than Earth could rotate so much faster on its axis! The rotational period of Jupiter is 9.841 hours!

and Saturn represent the different stages of human life from childhood up to old age, and they also indicate the moral and intellectual character of each one of these periods traversed by human beings. There are some Saturnians who are already old men at age 16, and there are some Mercurials who have the gaiety and the enthusiasm of childhood at 70. The Moon and Venus bring us the feminine in her two major modes: motherhood and love, and have respectively the white color of the pure water and the green color of the sea as their symbols.

Remember also that each day of the week corresponds to one of the seven planetary influences: Sundays to the Sun, Mondays to the Moon, Tuesdays to Mars, Wednesdays to Mercury, Thursdays to Jupiter, Fridays to Venus, and Saturdays to Saturn. Now you have the essence of viewing the stars from the magical point of view.

The Moon in the Twelve Signs

We arrive now at the survey of the connections of the Moon with the signs of zodiac. This is essential for the magician.

We know that every sign contains 30 degrees. For the ease of description in the following survey, we have divided, the signs into three portions: head, middle, and end, each one 10 degrees. We call upon the following traditions for our "key."[94]

---

[94] This system of dividing the zodiac into three sectors per sign is an Egyptian technique called the "decans" or "Faces." This was originally considered a form of essential dignity; however, Morinus, Papus' 17th-century French predecessor, began the process of disconnecting the so-called "minor" essential dignities. Morinus instead emphasized yet another usage of the decanates, which was more akin to their original use in Egypt and Mesopotamia. The original use of the decans was as time markers: 10 degrees of constellational sky was a calendric marker. Thus, from this period onward, the decans were recognized to possess unique qualities. By disconnecting them from the system of essential dignities, Morinus and his followers actually gave them higher status and importance, because as a dignity, the Face was largely overshadowed by the remaining sign rulership, Exaltation and

Aries (Degrees 1 to 30). The Moon at this time pours out very happy influences for commerce, and for the prosperity of travelers. The sacred inscriptions, talesmen who are formed under this influence, ward against dangers and perils for travelers and traders.

♈ *(Middle Degrees 10 to 20).* The Moon influences wealth and the discovery of treasures. The moment is favorable to make talesmen and characters in order to be lucky at gaming, mainly if the Moon is in a benign aspect with Jupiter (conjunction).

Taurus (Degrees 30 to 60). The influence on the characters and talismen leads toward the ruin of buildings, wells and fountains, to the rupture of the good will, or of marriages begun, and other similar things.

♉ *(Degree 60).* Twenty-five minutes after the exit from Taurus, the Moon influences happy health, a grand disposition to learn the sciences and to reconcile the kindliness of people of distinction, and if, at this time, it is in conjunction with Venus, the talismen and other figures that one makes under this constellation will be infallible to prompt a loving disposition in the fair sex.

Gemini (Degrees 60 to 90). Happy hunting, success in military enterprises. The influences of the Moon at this moment render insurmountable those that carry some talisman, mysterious figures, or characters formed under the auspices of this constellation.

Triplicity. We should also mention that there are two major Western systems of decanates known. The so-called "Chaldean decanates" (also known as the Faces) follow the Chaldean order of the planets. The cycle begins with the first decan or Face of Aries, given to Mars. The sequence follows: Sun, Venus (and in Taurus), Mercury, Moon, Saturn, etc. The other system uses the Triplicities or Elements to assign the rulers. Thus, for Aries we use the Fire Triplicity, so the three decans are Mars, Sun, and Jupiter, the rulers of Aries, Leo and Sagittarius, etc.

Cancer (Degrees 90 to 120). Malignant influences, success of treason, conspiracies, and other attempts. If yet the Moon is in fortunate aspect with Jupiter, Venus, and Mercury, the talisman will be favorable to love, to games of luck, and to the discovery of treasures.

Leo (Degrees 120 to 150). In aspect with Saturn, it has influence over all fatal enterprises from the beginning of its entrance into this sign. When leaving this sign (10 last degrees), this constellation is liberal in all sorts of prosperity.

Virgo (Degrees 150 to 180). Good influences, unless aspected with Saturn. The talismen and characters prepared under this constellation are very advantageous to players, travelers, as well as to those that aspire to great honors.

Libra (Degrees 180 to 210). Encourages treasure-hunting enterprises, the discovery of riches, mines of metals, and fertile sources for fountains.

Scorpio (Degrees 210 to 240). Very harmful for travelers, and to those that get married, or who are beginning something social.

Sagittarius (Degrees 240 to 270). Good influences for honors and the length of the life.

Capricorn (Degrees 270 to 300). Favored by a kindly beholding[95] of Venus or of Jupiter, the Moon here influences health

---

[95] Beholding is a common expression for denoting two conditions: either the planets are in aspect, or they are in antiscial or contra-antiscial relationship to each other. The antiscia are a system based on equal day or night length. The signs are paired around their distance from the solstice points of 0° Cancer or Capricorn. In the Northern Hemisphere, the longest day of the year is the Summer Solstice, represented astrologically as 0° Cancer. Moving away from this longest day, the next longest day would be given by the pair 29° Gemini and 1° Cancer; these degrees are antiscial, or solstice points. Similarly 28° Gemini, 2° Cancer. The sign pairs that cor-

as well as love of the fair sex, the fate of talismen and characters prepared under this constellation is to undo the aglet[96] infallibly and obstruct the malefics from harming the marriage, and to maintain friendship and good intelligence among married people.

Aquarius (Degrees 300 to 330). Bad influences for health and for journeys.

Pisces (Degrees 330 to 360). This is the only aspect of Saturn to fear for those who want to prepare some talismen and characters under this constellation; because, so long as it is beheld amiably by Jupiter, Mercury, or Venus, it infallibly influences games of luck.

Astrology and Embryology

The *Primum Mobile*, which contains within its daily movement all the inferior spheres, communicates virtue by its influence to the existing and moving matter: the sphere of the fixed stars deals not only power to the fetus to distinguish future figures and accidents, but also communicates the very power of differentiating, following the different influences of this sphere. The sphere of Saturn is immediately after the firmament, and the soul receives the discernment and reason of this planet; then the one of Jupiter that gives the soul generosity and several other passions. Mars communicates hate, anger, and a lot of other emotions; the Sun influences science and memory; Venus the movements of sexual desire; Mercury joy and pleasure; finally the Moon, who is the origin of all the natural virtues, fortifies it. Some things come from the

---

respond in this fashion are Gemini-Cancer, Taurus-Leo, Aries-Virgo, Pisces-Libra, Aquarius-Scorpio, and Capricorn-Sagittarius. The contra-antiscion is the sign opposite the antiscial sign: so the contra-antiscion of 1° Cancer is 29° Sagittarius.
[96] The metal tip that can be placed on the end of a thread to facilitate threading.

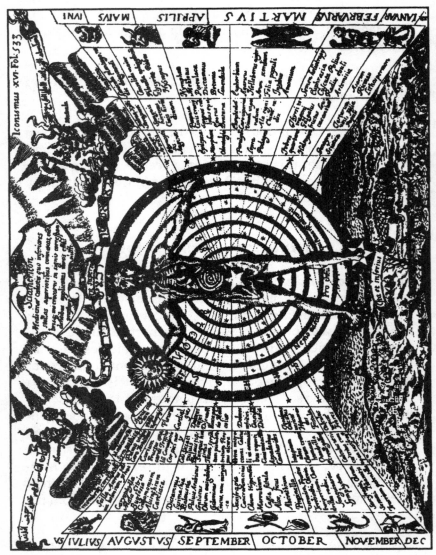

Figure 24. Astrological and Hermetic correspondences of the human body (after Kircher)

soul, and the soul has received into itself several components from the celestial bodies; however one assigns them: to everybody, or to the arrows of fate, because one simple accident is not sufficient to sustain them all.

Physical Body

Now, let's consider the body created and formed from the embryo by the effects and the operations of stars that we call the planets. It is necessary to understand that the matter from which human beings are created, being taken and tightened by the coldness and dryness of *Saturn*, receives an invigorating and vegetative virtue from this planet. There are two strengths in Saturn: the one of preparing matter generally, and the other of giving it a particular kind of shape.

Saturn dominates in the conception of the embryo during the first month. *Jupiter* takes a turn in the second, and by a special favor and a singular virtue, disposes the matter to both take and receive the members that the body must have. Saturn reinforces the same members. Jupiter also reinforces the matter of the fetus with a marvelous heat, and dampens all the parts which were dried by Saturn in the first month.

During the third month, *Mars*, with its heat, makes the head, and then distinguishes all the members from each other; for example, it separates the neck from the arms, the arms from the sides, and thus, in succession.

The *Sun*, dominant in the fourth month, imprints the different shapes upon the fetus. It creates the heart, and quickens the sensitive soul, if we believe the [ancient] physicians and astronomers. Aristotle is of another opinion and maintains that the heart is begotten before all the other parts, and that it is from it that they develop. Some others, wanting to up the ante, say that it is the Sun who is the source and the origin of the life.

Venus, in the fifth month, perfects by its influence the external members, and forms some others like the ears, the nose, the bones, the penis and foreskin in males, the matrix or the vulva and the breasts in females. In addition, it separates and distinguishes the hands, feet, and fingers.

During the sixth month, under the domination and the influence of *Mercury*, the organs of the voice, eyebrows, and eyes are formed. Under the influence of the same planet, hair grows, and the nails become visible on the fetus.

The *Moon* finishes, in the seventh month, that which was begun by the other planets, because it fills with its wetness all the empty spaces within the flesh. *Venus and Mercury dampen all the body, giving nurturance as necessary.*

We assign the eighth month to Saturn who, by its influence, cools and dries much of the fetus and therefore tightens it. But Jupiter, who reigns in the ninth, gladdens the fetus by its heat and humidity.

Adaptations to Medicine

In one of his studies of astral influences, Flambart expresses the following:

> Having given the correspondences of various illnesses with specific astral influences, one must conclude that, if they are not the source, properly speaking, of illnesses, they offer, nonetheless, some indicator correspondences of which medicine would do well at times to avail itself like diagnosis and prognosis. There is no doubt that the Native's predisposition toward health, often very clear in the horoscope, is of a type to interest the physician concerning the kind of attention to give to the sick person; and much more so, I believe, for determining, with a certain precision, the nature and degree of morbid receptiveness of every individual, according to the heavens at the moment of birth.[97]

---

[97] Papus doesn't credit this quote; it may be from C. Flammarion's *Popular Astronomy*.

We saw already (on page 101) how every planetary influence contributes to form a part of our body, and how every sign of the zodiac is in correspondence, not only with the various parts of body, but also with the various creatures of the mineral and plant kingdoms.

One sees, therefore, in succession, that a plant influenced by Jupiter, having concentrated a part of this special strength of the invisible energy in itself, will heal an illness of a part of the body in correspondence with the same force, etc.

A physician of great value, Dr. Duz, attempted to adapt the data of traditional astrology to medicine, based strictly on his experience. In order to give readers an idea of the methods that could be adapted from astrological knowledge in medicine, while remaining within the limits of our survey, which constitutes a beginning or initiation only, we will give an outline of the Moon's action in the twelve zodiacal signs, and a summary of the physiological and pathological action that Dr. Duz' experience allowed him to note.

Action of the Moon

The Moon has a continuous action on beings and on things, and its transition through the twelve zodiacal signs influences the human body in the following manner:

In Aries: It assigns the encephalic nervous system, the head and its dependencies, and forms the hepatic diathesis.[98]
Elementary Qualities: hot and dry.

---

[98] "Diathesis" is a slightly archaic wording. The concept that Papus is discussing is basically predisposition to disease: the idea that the Moon's sign gives the type somatic weakness to which the individual is prone. This weakness tends to be found in particular organs, resulting in particular patterns of disease or syndrome. We should add that these particular attributions do not necessarily correspond to those given in the usual astrological sources, such as Cornell.

In Taurus: The Moon rules the glandular system and thyroid, hypophysis, neck, throat, and their dependencies, and forms the renal diathesis.
Elementary Qualities: dry and cold.

In Gemini: The Moon rules the respiratory system (superior, right and left lobes of the lungs), the pulmonary innervation, the superior members of body, and the dorsal vertebras 1, 2, 3, 4, and forms the cranial diathesis.
Elementary Qualities: hot and humid.

In Cancer: The Moon rules the digestive organs (stomach, epigastric, and their dependencies), the diaphragm, the lower lobes (right 2 lobes, left 1 lobe of the lungs) and the pleura, and forms the [cranial] abdominal diathesis.
Elementary Qualities: cold and humid.

In Leo: The Moon assigns the cardiac system and circulatory (heart, major vessels), the first third superior of the stomach and the cardia, the dorsal vertebrae 5, 6, 7, 8, 9, and forms the cardiac diathesis.
Elementary Qualities: hot and dry.

In Virgo: The Moon affects the second third right inferior of the stomach, the solar plexus, the pyloric valve, the left lobe of the liver and the lobule of Spigel, the pancreas and their dependencies, the abdominal epigastric system and all its dependencies, and forms the cranial diathesis.
Elementary Qualities: dry and cold.

In Libra: The Moon affects the loins, the umbilical region right and left, and the hypogastric area; that is to say, the inguinal regions right and left, a part of the small intestines, the bladder in children, and the uterus in time of pregnancy, and forms the renal diathesis.
Elementary Qualities: hot and humid.

In Scorpio: The Moon affects the genital-urinary systems,

the bladder, the matrix, the hypophysis and the other sanguine vascular glands, and forms the hepatic diathesis.
Elementary Qualities: humid and cold .

In Sagittarius: The Moon affects the muscular system and
also the heart, blood vessels, the gastro-intestinal lining,
vesical muscle, the lumbar region and thighs, and forms the
thoracic diathesis.
Elementary Qualities: hot and dry.

In Capricorn: The Moon affects the cutaneous and mucous
systems, the cellular tissue, the knees, and forms the splenic
diathesis.
Elementary Qualities: dry and cold.

In Aquarius: The Moon affects the blood system (the blood);
the legs, ankle bones, and forms the splenic diathesis.
Elementary Qualities: hot and humid.

In Pisces: The Moon affects the fibro-ligamentous synovial
and respiratory systems; the heel-bone, the feet, and forms
the thoracic diathesis.
Elementary Qualities: humid and cold.

The following list mentions planetary influences from the
point of view of physiological and pathological action.

1 Mars Group
    1 Encephalic nervous system and cerebro-spinal or life
      of native;
    2 Organs of the head;
    3 Genital-urinary system and renal;
    4 Vascular sanguine glands;
    5 Inflammation, stenia;[99]
    6 Localizations, lesions.

---

[99] i.e., unusual level of activity or vigor.

2 *Venus Group*
   1 Glandular systems, thyroid, and naso-pharyngeal;
   2 Renal and hepatic systems;
   3 Humoral secretions;
   4 Dystrophy;
   5 Infectious illnesses.

3 *Saturn Group*
   1 Cutaneous and bony system;
   2 Blood system (blood and its composition);
   3 Cellular tissue;
   4 Mucous tissue;
   5 Debility or organic weakness;
   6 Chronicity;
   7 Stenose.

4 *Jupiter Group*
   1 Muscular systems and fibro-ligaments reaching the
     pulmonary parenchyme, the blood vessels, the car-
     diac muscle, the gastro-intestinal lining, the vesicular
     muscle;
   2 Poisoning, dyscrasia;
   3 Lower members.

5 *Mercury Group*
   1 Chylification, gastro-abdominal innervation (solar
     plexus and its branchings);
   2 Sanguification and pulmonary innervation (brachial
     plexus);
   3 Neurosis;
   4 Metastasy;
   5 Superior members.

6 *Moon Group*
   1 Nutrition for life (grand sympathetic), reaching all
     the organic systems;
   2 Periodicity;

3 Microzymase;
4 Sharp state;
5 Hyperemia.

7 *Sun Group*
1 Circulatory blood system;
2 Vital strength;
3 Tonicity;
4 Irritation;
5 State of panic.

Ignorance of astrology makes it impossible to understand anything about the occult sciences, the splendid inheritance from extinct civilizations. We understand that modern science could benefit from its acquaintance, and that medicine, among others, could find great benefit in the application of planetary or zodiacal correspondences. The study of the mineral, plant, animal, and human kingdoms can be much facilitated if we are acquainted with the connections between the astral forces and the innumerable creatures who evolve on the Earth toward their common source: God, their creator.

I am persuaded that the seven planetary forces and the twelve zodiacal forces constitute a preferable classification to those adopted by modern science. The various colors of plants, for example, are very revealing for those that know.

But let's remain within the limits of this totally elementary study and set boundaries by indicating, in Table 4 on page 108, the action of the seven planets on human beings in determining a temperament and a particular character. Table 5 (page 109) gives the favorite color for each planetary type. We will finish with Table 6, listing some of the influences some planets on nature (pages 110–111).Also note figure 25 borrowed from Desbarolles (p. 112), the famous palmist, for it indicates the localizations in the hand of the planetary influences.

Now that we have combined the complete study of zodiacal and planetary forces in the previous chapters, we can

Table 4. The Names of the Seven Planets with the Seven
Corresponding Temperaments, and the Seven Character
Types which Depend of these Seven Temperaments.

PLANET	QUALITY	TEMPERAMENT	CHARACTER
Saturn	Duration Time	Bilious	Slow, cold, reflexive, intelligent, thinking.
Jupiter	Beneficent	Blood- Bilious	Quick, settled, frank and faithful, intelligent, imperious, domineering.
Mars	Impetuous	Muscular	Boiling, impatient, loss of control, violent.
Venus	Housemaid "Come Hither"	Nervous- Blood- Lymphatic	Soft, under-standing, good, nice to the weak.
Mercury	Agile	Nervous- Bilious	Intelligent design, skillful, artful.
Moon	Soft	Lymphatic	Soft, mobile imagination, changing.
Sun	Brilliant	Harmonic	Ideal, big, gen-erous, friend of beautiful, powerful in artistic creations.

Table 5. Correspondences of Seven Colors with Principal
Temperaments and Characters; Showing the Favorite
Color of Each with the Name of the Planet that Rules it.

TEMPERAMENT	CHARACTER	FAVORITE COLOR	PLANET
Bilious	Serious, A thinker	Yellow-orange	Saturn
Blood	Jovial, Loud, Domineering	Red	Jupiter
Nervous	Sentimental, Magnetic	Blue	Venus
Nervous bilious	Design, Skillful, Artful	Green	Mercury
Blood muscular	Violent, Loss of control, Brutal	Brown (bistro or blood red)	Mars
Lymphatic	Soft, Slow, Fickle, Shy, Modest	Purple	Moon
Solar harmonic	Big, Generous, An artist	Light or gold	Sun

Table 6. Influence of the Planets.

PLANET	MUSICAL NOTE	METALS	COLOR	PRECIOUS STONES	FLOWERS OR PLANTS	ANIMALS
Neptune	—	[Electrum]	Mauve	—	—	—
Uranus	—	Platinum	Striped or mixed	—	—	—
Saturn	La	Lead	Black Brown	Jet, onyx Dark coral	Aconite, Amaranths, Ivy, Holly, Moss, Great Christmas rose, Poplar	Dog, Snake
Jupiter	Fa	Tin	Crimson Purple	Amethyst, Emerald, Dark Sapphire, Turquoise	Geranium, Stock, Marjolaine, Hyssop,Lark, Eyelets, Jasmine	Eagle, Peacock, Deer, Lark, Partridge
Mars	Sol	Iron	Red blood	Ruby, Garnet, Red chalk, Carnelian	Aloe, Anemone [gieull] Peony, Dahlia, Broom, Panicle, Barberry, Fuchsia, Hops, Rhubarb, Tobacco	Horse, Tiger, Vulture, Rooster, Green woodpecker

Table 6. Influence of the Planets (continued).

Sun	Do	Gold	Yellow Orange	Amber, Chrysolite, Topaz	Helianthus, Heliotrope, Century, Mistletoe, Saffron, Lemon, Camomile, Orange tree	Lion, Goat, Ram, Canary
Venus	Re	Copper	Blue Rose	Beryl, Aquamarine, Clear sapphire, Coral, Rose, Lapis lazuli	Lily of the valley, Narcissus, Roses, Lily, Seringa, Jasmine, Violets, Pansy, Foxglove, Tansy, Daisies, Elder, Hyacinths	Sparrow, Wood pigeon, Nightingale, Turtledove
Mercury	Si	Quicksilver	Azure Light Blue	Marcasite, Tigers eye Agate, Jasper, Colored stones	Lavender, Mint, Vervain, Valerian, Balm-mint, Bindweed, Germander, Annuals, Anise, Daisies	Magpie, Linnet, Swallow, Butterflies, Parrot
Moon	Mi	Silver	Blue Gray White	Diamond, Pearls, Crystal, Selenite, Labrador	Mallows, Water-lily, Poppy, Forget-me-not, Clovers, Saxifrage	Cat, Osprey, Bat, Butterflies of evening

Figure 25.   Planetary influences in the hand.

now understand clearly that not only is Astrology really the universal key to Magic, Alchemy, divinatory sciences and of all the mysterious sciences of the Past, but that it constitutes, as well, the basis for the synthesis of the sciences so cherished in the profane world. This synthesis has already arrived for those who know how to handle this precious instrument.

If, therefore, readers who seriously study these pages refer to this work in making the resolution to deepen the study of astrology within themselves, my goal will be reached and I will be extensively rewarded for the work I have done.

APPENDIX

ASTROLOGY AND THE CALENDAR

Definitive reform of the Calendar

THE CALENDAR IS THE FRIEND of the houses, our
guide to the trails of existence.

Each one of us daily consults this guide, receives this
friend to our table, but who among us thinks of controlling
the signs of this guide? Who worries about these interce-
dents, who is concerned about the origin and the character
of this friend? Who finally suspects that we have a decep-
tive guide and are poorly informed by our calendar, which
is a fantastic friend but not very respectable?

In our innocence, we have all believed that the calendar
records faithfully all the movements of the Sun, the Moon
and the Earth; that the division of the year into twelve
months answered to the movements of the Moon; that the
division of day in twenty-four hours was logical, etc.

Hey well! Nothing of the kind!

Our calendar doesn't record the revolutions accomplished by our planet around the Sun: it only records the returns of the seasons. It is not the same thing at all, because,
in the time it takes for the return of the seasons 25,765 times,
the Earth makes only 25,764 revolutions around the Sun.

Our calendar no longer records the rotations accomplished by our planet around its axis; it records the returns
of the Sun to the meridian only; that is to say, the return of
the hours. It is not the same thing because, in the time
wherein the hours return 365 times, the Earth turns 366
times on its axis.

Hitherto, nevertheless, there is not anything to retell.
Our calendar is right. Indeed, we don't need to know how
many times the Earth turns, or doesn't turn, upon itself or
around the Sun, but we need to know in every instant

where we are with the march of the seasons and of the hours. These last facts adjust all the business of our lives, all the habits of our existence.

If we started to count the revolutions of the Earth around the Sun by *sidereal* years of a length of 365 days, 6 hours, 9 minutes, 11 seconds, instead of counting the return of the seasons or counting by the tropical year, of a middle length of 365 days, 5 hours, 48 minutes, 45 seconds, we would soon see the seasons advance on the times fixed by the calendar. We would have to adjust this.

The same thing would happen if we started to count the rotations of the Earth on itself (or by *sidereal* days 23 hours, 56 minutes, 4 seconds) in place of counting the returns of the hours or by mean days of 24 hours. We would soon see the Sun rise and set at hours increasingly incorrect. Now, as the Sun would not be inconvenienced in order to be in synch with our clocks, it would be necessarily better that we inconvenienced our clocks to put them in synch with the Sun, and we would have to reset our clocks frequently.

Our calendar also lacks a reason to begin the year on January 1st. This mistake, however, is not inexcusable. At the beginning of this century, Earth was regularly at the closest point to the Sun on January 1st, the point named the *perihelion*. That day could be considered to be the real beginning of the year, because it is veritably *the birthday of the birth* of the Earth. Our globe celebrates it like a devoted son leaving the most faraway regions in order to return home to his mother every year.

Unfortunately the Earth doesn't arrive at the perihelion on January 1st anymore. Since 1876, it arrives at perihelion on January 3. In 1932, it will arrive on the 4th of January, and thus in succession, every 56 years, one day later.

Our new year should actually begin on the winter solstice, December 21, because this point marks the extreme limits of the obliquity of the solar rays; that is to say, the precise end of the tropical or meteorological year and the beginning of a new one. We could object that, if the winter solstice is the best point of departure of the year for us, the summer solstice will be the best for the inhabitants of the opposite hemisphere to ours, but this objection loses all its value as soon as we consider that our hemisphere carries nearly the totality of the inhabitable Earth. The boreal hemisphere was, and always will be, the main theater of our destinies, and certainly, if one of the two must make the law for the other—as is the case here—it is the boreal hemisphere, the most ancient, that must order, and the southern, the younger, that must obey.

The calendar makes a less excusable mistake when it takes away the leap days from three secular years in the fourth.

The tropical year, let us recall, lasts a mean of 365 days, 5 hours, 48 minutes, and 45 seconds. It takes 365 days and a quarter, to nearly 675 seconds.*

The ancients, who knew the length of the year only by the number of its days, naturally didn't count this incomplete quarter of a day. Their year was too short, and advanced more and more upon the seasons. One could see this from the time of Julius Caesar. Under the reign of this emperor, the calendar was reformed, and humans began to count one extra day in the year every four years in order to recapture the four quarters lost in the interval.

Later, in 1583, when people had arrived at a more

---

* The length of the tropical year depends on some variations which take place as a result of the eccentricity of the terrestrial orbit. The Parisian astronomers have reached little agreement on this length during various times in history and therefore on the assessment of its mean.

C. Flammarion (*Popular Astronomy*, p. 34) said that at the beginning of this century, the length of the tropical year was of 365 days, 5 hours, 48 minutes, 51 seconds. C. Pilloy (*Lessons of Astronomy*, 1877) assigns a present length of 365 days, 5 hours, 48 minutes, 47 seconds. We understand that with such information, it is difficult to come to the right idea. We established our mean on some theoretical bases entirely independent of the observation and astronomical calculations. Now, it agrees with the data of most authors. The difference, when it would be wrong by several seconds, would not result in an appreciable gap to the march of the seasons in a remote time well beyond the likely end of history.

press acquaintance of the length of the tropical year, they recognized that the remedy employed against the advance of the calendar had been too strong, and that it was now necessary to delay it .

These 675 seconds, counted four times too much every leap year, made, by their accumulation since the beginning of the vulgar era, 12 days too many.

1582 × years 675 seconds = 1,064,686 seconds = 12 days.

They therefore reformed the calendar anew. It was Pope Gregory VII, who helped the astronomers of his time, who accomplished it. October 5, 1582 became the 15th in all the Catholic countries (one will see later why the 15th and not the 17th) and in order to prevent the reoccurrence of this difference, they resolved to suppress the leap days of three centennial years out of four.

So, there was no 6, 7, 8, 9, 10, 11, 12, 13 and 14 October 1582 in history, and the years 1700, 1800, 1900 are leap years in the *Julian* calendar, but not anymore in the *Gregorian*.

At the point where we arrived at this historic moment, we find ourselves scrutinizing with an attentive eye the works of our forefathers and discovering with stupefaction that after all the remedies and contra-remedies, the calendar advances again today as it advanced in the time of Julius Caesar. The gap is not the same anymore, it is true, but it is no less real.

To prevent a delay, increasing by reason of 675 seconds per year, it was not necessary to suppress one leap day all 133-1/3 years—following three in 400 years—but all the 128. We get the number 133-1/3 when we take the length of the tropical year for a basis as it was in 1582 that is to say: 365 days, 5 hours, 49 minutes, 12 seconds or 365 days and a quarter, less 688 seconds. The calculation is easy:

There are 86,400 seconds in one day's time{ 86.400: 675
= 128.
86.400: 648 = 133.33, etc.

The Gregorian calendar will therefore be early by one day in 11,200 years time. Certainly it is not that mistake which will ever put us in disagreement with the march of the seasons and which renders necessary a new reform; also we wouldn't speak of it, if it was not a part of a *system* of mistakes that distorts all our calendars and renders reform indispensable.

This system consists of substituting a sound notation for reality based on metaphysical dreams born of an imperfect consideration of the numbers and destitute of all philosophical certainty, of all scientific guarantee. These conceptions are not anything other than vague apprehensions, some dark presentiments of the law of definitive creation henceforth settled on a philosophical basis and scientifically unshakable.

See the effects of this disastrous system.

When we first examine the Gregorian reform, the conclusion that first comes to mind is that the astronomers of the 16th century didn't know the variations which take place in the eccentricity of the terrestrial orbit, and therefore they didn't calculate the mean length of the tropical year—the mean which should have served as the basis for their reform.

A deeper examination shows that in all cases the adopted basis was preferred to all others because it seemed to offer advantages that none of the others did. What were these advantages?

It didn't appear so much that it was a question of correcting the advance of the Roman calendar. Indeed, if we take a yearly advance of 675 seconds or an advance of 648 seconds as the basis of calculation, the correction made remains the same appreciably. It is 12 full days in the first case; 11 days, 20 hours, 57 minutes, 16 seconds—is 12 days less 3 hours, 12 minutes, 44 seconds in the second. (October 5 1582 would have therefore been called the 17th or the 16th, rather than the 15th. One called it the 15th because it was more convenient. There was only to put 1 before the number 5 and all was said and done. The voluntary mistake that one committed was of a remainder without consequence.)

The advantages in question appeared when they were about to prevent the return to the uncorrected advance. Indeed:

In distinguishing under the name of *centennial* the designated years by hundreds and in depriving leap years in three out of four of these years, one reproduced "in macro," that is to say, on a ladder of 400 years the mechanics served "in micro," that is to say on a ladder of 4 years, in order to purge the amount of time; in this way the working of macro-mechanics also became easy to adjust and to keep for micro-mechanics. The group of four purified years are arranged in good order with the group of four purified centennials. It was simple, logical and compliant to the *decimal* numeration, the only one known.

But on what foundation does this distinction rest between centennial and non-centennial years?

The result indicates or allows us to suppose that a set of one hundred years forms any kind of reality to which one can logically give the name of "century?"

The bewildered reader believes that we joke! Not at all! The question could not be more seriously posed, and we challenge anyone to at least make a reasonable answer.

We use the name "year" for the set of 365 days. Nothing better. This set corresponds to the reality of a revolution accomplished by the Earth around the Sun. But what happens in the sky or on the Earth, in the mind of the observer, anywhere, when the year slips away—that one designated by the number of one hundred, a number which begins a new series of numbers. We are going to pierce the veil of this mystery.

The Romans, to whom we give the invention of the "bisextile" day and who gave the name "two-horned" to distinguish it again today, placed this day at the end of their year, appointed as March 1st. (This name is from the God of

War [Mars]—a pretty beginning of the year. This was promised for New Year's gifts.) Placed thus between two years, as it should indeed be, the leap day formed of four incomplete quarters doesn't represent rigorously the end the year that it follows nor the beginning of the one that it precedes. It belongs to four incomplete quarters[†] for the year which precedes it and for the remaining[*] to the year which follows it.

It is—in all the strength of the term—one *middle* day, and as it serves to "purify," we will name it "lustral."

The middle lustral, therefore, considered positively, that is to say as belonging *partially* to first the one and then the other year between which it is found, indissolubly *welds* these two years together and makes of two years of 365 days one duplicate of 731 days.

Considered negatively on the contrary, that is to say, as not belonging *fully* to one year nor to the other of the two years that it welds together, but to the group of four of years of which it purges the advance, and as having all the groups of four years that it slows down, the middle lustral welds all these groups of four one to the other and makes of all the set, as far as the soldering spreads, one reality to which it is acceptable to give the name of century, if this word, like some etymologists believes, means *following of years* (Latin *sequi*, to follow) or if, like some others think, it means *time of the life* (Gaëlic *saoghal*).

Therefore, one real century is a set of 32 groups of four years, welded successively one to the other and finally to a 33rd group of four which purifies them all by the suppression of one day. The suppression of this day— which would have been a middle—interrupts the soldering and determines the end of one century, the beginning of another.

---

† That is, 23 hours and a quarter.
* That is, three quarters of an hour.

Things to Consider for
the Explanation of the Calendar

We can finally bring back to four key points all the relative subjects of the calendar, of which the previous discussion was necessary for understanding, and in order to develop its origin and its reasoning.

1. The stars were used to adjust the calendar, the Sun and the Moon, the five other planets, the twelve signs of the zodiac, some remarkable constellations and by their shape, and because their rising and setting agrees with the various works of the countryside, such: Orion, the Pleiades, the Canis Major or the Big Dog, etc.

2. The various parts of time, which show the effect of the revolutions of these stars and which compose the year as: the day, in the night, the hours, the weeks, the months, the seasons.

3. The length of the year and the principal combinations that one made of the years to form their own cycles to reconcile the various movements of the Sun and of the Moon.

4. The days of the year which used to divide into months and into seasons; such as, New Year's Day, the first of every month or the New Moons, the Solstices, and the Equinoxes, which adjust the four seasons, or the four times. The distribution of these days into happy and unhappy, the assemblies, markets, fairs, etc., which take place throughout the calendar.

The Year of every Planet

The Earth takes 365 days to turn around the Sun, and it is to that which we assign the Sun himself this movement. It is the time of coming back to the astronomical reality, such at least as it is currently taught.

Let us consider the length in terrestrial days of the year of every planet.

Going away from the Sun:

Mercury	87.969 days[100]
Venus	224.701 days
The Earth	365.256 days
Mars	686.98 days
Jupiter	11.8623 years
Saturn	29.458 years
Uranus	84.01 years
Neptune	164.79 years
[Pluto	248.54 years]

One sees by these numbers that one night of Saturn lasts thirty times longer than the time of a terrestrial night or that the inhabitants of Saturn sleep one month in succession and stay up one month in succession with regard to terrestrial time.

Once again, one will find in the elementary books of astronomy all that concerns the density, the mass, the distance to the Sun and the other physical details of every planet.

The poet Manilius described the manner of character of each of the twelve signs.[101]

Now constellations, Muse, and signs rehearse;
In order let them sparkle in thy verse;
First Aries, glorious in his golden wool,
Looks back, and wonders at the mighty Bull,
Whose hind parts first appear, he bending lies,

---

[100] I have corrected these numbers to represent the current values, and added a value for Pluto.

[101] And so Papus concludes by even borrowing his final quote from Burgoyne, who gave it as his opening to Volume 1, Chapter 6. We give Burgoyne's text here.

With threatening head, then calls the Twins to rise;
They clasp for fear, and mutually embrace,
And next the Twins with an unsteady pace
Bright Cancer rolls; then Leo shakes his mane
And following Virgo calms his rage again.
Then night and day are weighed in Libra's scales,
Equal awhile, at last the night prevails;
And longer grown the heavier scale inclines,
And draws bright Scorpio from the winter signs.
Him Centaur follows with an aiming eye,
His bow full drawn and ready to let fly;
Next narrow horns, the twisted Caper shows,
And from Aquarius' urn a flood o'er flows.
Near their lov'd waves cold Pisces takes their seat,
With Aries join, and make the round complete.

Centaur, the constellation of Jupiter, i.e., Sagittarius.
Narrow-horns, the twisted Caper, refers to Capricorn, the goat."

TABLES

These tables have been added by translator to clarify information presented in the text.

Table 1.   Essential Dignities and Debilities.*

SIGN	DOMICILE (+5)	EXALTATION (+4)	DETRIMENT (−5)	FALL (−4)
♈	♂	☉	♀	♄
♉	♀	☽	♂	
♊	☿	☊	♃	☋
♋	☽	♃	♄	♂
♌	☉		♄	
♍	☿	☿	♃	♀
♎	♀	♄	♂	☉
♏	♂		♀	☽
♐	♃	☋	☿	☊
♑	♄	♂	☽	♃
♒	♄		☉	
♓	♃	♀	☿	☿

*Whole sign types. Point values given per William Lilly, *Christian Astrology* (1647; Reprinted Regulus: London, 1985), p. 104.

Table 2.   Triplicities from Ptolemy and Lilly.*

SIGN	PTOLEMY: DAY	PTOLEMY: NIGHT	PTOLEMY: MIXED	LILLY: DAY	LILLY: NIGHT
♈ ♌ ♐	☉	♃	♂	☉	♃
♉ ♍ ♑	♀	☽	♄	♀	☽
♊ ♎ ♒	♄	☿	♃	♄	☿
♋ ♏ ♓	♀	♃	♂	♂	♂

*Point value is +3 for chosen type. From William Lilly, *Christian Astrology* (1647; Reprinted Regulus: London, 1985), p. 104.

Table 3. Accidental Dignities and Debilities.*

ACCIDENTAL DIGNITIES		ACCIDENTAL DEBILITIES	
In the MC or Ascendant	5	In the 12th house	−5
In the 7th/4th/11th houses	4	In the 8th/6th house	−2
In the 2nd/5th houses	3	Retrograde	−5
In the 9th house	2	Slow in Motion	−2
In the 3rd house	1	♄ ♃ ♂ Occidental	−2
Direct (except ☉ and ☽)	4	♀ ☿ Oriental	−2
Swift in Motion	2	☽ decreasing in light	−2
♄ ♃ ♂ Oriental	2	Combust of the ☉	−5
♀ ☿ Occidental	2	Under the ☉ Beams	−4
☽ increasing in light, or			
Occidental	2	Partile ☌ with ♄ or ♂	−5
Free from combustion			
and ☉ Beams	5	Partile ☌ with ☋	−4
Cazimi	5	Besieged of ♄ with ☋	−5
Partile ☌ with ♃ or ♀	5	Partile ☍ with ♄ or ♂	−4
Partile ☌ with ☊	4	Partile □ with ♄ or ♂	−3
Partile △ with ♃ or ♀	4	In ☌ or within 5° of	
		Caput Algol	−5
Partile ✶ with ♃ or ♀	3	– – –	
In ☌ with *Cor Leonis*	6	– – –	
In ☌ with Spica	5	– – –	

*Material compiled from William Lilly, *Christian Astrology* (1647; Reprinted Regulus: London, 1985), p. 115; and Claudius Ptolemy, *Tetrabiblos*, translated by F. E. Robbins (second century A.D.; Harvard University Press: Cambridge, 1971), pp. 82–87.

TRANSLATOR'S REFERENCES

Blagrave, Joseph. 1671. *Astrological Practice of Physick*. Obad. Blagrave: London. Available from Ballantrae.

Burgoyne, Thomas. 1889. *The Light of Egypt*. Published 1889 by Religio-Philosophical Publishing House, San Francisco, 1889. Reissued in 1963 by H. O. Wagner, Denver, CO.

Choisnard, Paul. 1925, 1983. *Saint Thomas d'Aquin et l'Influence des Astres*. Éditions Traditionnelles: Paris.

Curry, Patrick. 1992. *A Confusion of Prophets: Victorian and Edwardian Astrology*. Collins & Brown: London.

Dariot, Claude. 1653. *A Brief Introduction conducing to the Judgment of the Stars, wherein the whole Art of Judiciall Astrologie is briefly and plainly delivered*. Translated by Fabian Withers and enlarged by Nathaniel Spark. London.

Godwin, Joscelyn. 1994. *The Theosophical Enlightenment*. State University Press of New York: Albany.

Godwin, Joscelyn, Christian Chanel, and John P. Deveney. 1995. *The Hermetic Brotherhood of Luxor*. Samuel Weiser: York Beach, ME.

Gould, Stephen Jay. 1981. *The Mismeasure of Man*. W. W. Norton: New York.

Knappish, Wilhelm. 1967, 1986. *Histoire de l'Astrologie*. Translated by Henri Latou. Vernal: Philippe Lebaud.

Kramer, Peter D. 1993. *Listening to Prozac*. Viking: New York.

Kuhn, Thomas S. 1962, 1970. *The Structure of Scientific Revolutions*. The University of Chicago Press: Chicago.

Lehman, J. Lee. 1989. *Essential Dignities*. Whitford Press: Atglen, PA.

——————. 1992. *The Book of Rulerships*. Whitford Press: Atglen, PA.

——————. 1996. *Classical Astrology for Modern Living*. Whitford Press: Atglen, PA.

Levy, Raphael. 1939. *The Beginning of Wisdom: An Astrological Treatise by Abraham ibn Ezra. An English Translation of the Hebrew Original*. The Johns Hopkins Press: Baltimore.

Lilly, William. 1647. *Christian Astrology*. Reprinted in 1985 by Regulus: London. Also available: Just Us & Associates: Issaquah, WA.

Little, Lucy. 1974. *Astrosynthesis: The Rational System of Horoscope Interpretation According to Morin de Villefranche*. Zoltan Mason, Emerald Books: New York

Mackey, Samson Arnold. 1822, 1973. *"Mythological" Astronomy of the Ancients Demonstrated*. Wizards Bookshelf: Minneapolis.

Morin, Jean Baptiste (also known as Morinus). 1661. *Astrologia Gallica Principiis et Rationibus propriis stabilita atque in XXVI Libros distributa, Nonsolum Astrologiae Judiciariae Studiosis, sed etiam Philosophis, Medicis, et Theologis monibus per necessaria*. Hagae-Comitis.

Papus. 1967. *The Tarot of the Bohemians*, trans. A. P. Morton, with a preface by A. E. Waite. Samuel Weiser: New York.

Potterton, David, ed. 1983. *Culpeper's Color Herbal.* Sterling Publishing Co.: New York.

Ptolemy, Claudius. 2nd century A.D. 1971. *Tetrabiblos.* Translated by F. E. Robbins. Harvard University Press: Cambridge.

Ramesey, William. 1653. *Astrologia Restaurata; or Astrology Restored: being an Introduction to the General and Chief part of the Language of the Stars.* Printed for Robert White: London.

Schwickert, Friedreich "Sinbad" and Adolf Weiss. 1972. *Cornerstones of Astrology.* Sangreal Foundation: Dallas.

Star, Ély. 1888. *Les mystères de l'Horoscope.* E. Dentu: Paris.

Weiss, Adolpho. 1946, 1987. *Astrologia Racional.* Editorial Kier S. A.: Buenos Aires.

INDEX

Pisces, 60, 79
  Intellectual Plane, 80
  Physical Plane, 80
planets, 9, 23
  combust, 24
  minor, 14
  seven, 18
Pollux, 65
Primum Mobile, 99
Ptolemy, 3

R
Ramesey, William, ix
Raphael I, x, 42
Rempha, 81
Reuben, 78
Ring, Thomas, xvi
ruby, 68

S
Sagittarius, 60, 74
  Intellectual Plane, 75
  Physical Plane, 75
St. John, 76
sapphire, sky blue, 78, 83
sardonix, 83
Saturn, 15, 19, 23, 25, 26,
  28–31, 33, 95
  Intellectual plane, 31
  Physical plane, 31
Saunders, Richard, ix
Schwickert, Friedreich, xvi
Scorpio, 59, 72
  Intellectual Plane, 73
  Physical Plane, 74
seasons, four, 5
Selva, Henri, xv, xvi, 89

Shebo, 30
Shenim, 44
signs, angular, 52
Simeon and Levi, 65
sky, divisons of, 2
solstice, winter, 52
South Node, 22
Star, Ely, xi
stars, 1
  stationary, 2
Sun, 10, 11, 19, 28, 37, 94
  Intellectual Plane, 38
  Physical Plane, 39
  under the beams of,
    25
Suroth, 81
system
  Copernican, 10
  Ptolemaic, 11

T
Tarot, 30
Taurus, 58, 63, 98
  Intellectual Plane, 64
  Physical Plane, 64
Theosophical Society, ix, xi
Thor, 32
de Titus, Placido, ix
topaz, 73, 83
triplicities, 83, 84, 125
  Airy, 86
  Earthly, 85
  Fire, 85
  four, 84
  Watery, 86
twelve signs, 47
Typhone, 82

J. Lee Lehman is a well-known author and activist in the astrological world, publishing such varied works as *The Ultimate Asteroid Book*, *Essential Dignities*, *The Book of Rulerships*, and *Classical Astrology for Modern Living*, and numerous articles that bridge the gap between classical and modern astrology. She received the 1995 Marc Edmund Jones Award, the first Horary astrologer so honored. Lehman heads the Classical Studies in Horary Course, the Introduction to Classical Astrology Course, and is co-founder of the Classical Studies in Electional Astrology. She has been a member of the National Council for Geocosmic Research, serving as National Research Director and Chair of the Executive Committee, and has been involved with the internationally known United Astrology Congress, serving as both Program Chair (in 1995, shared with Jim Lewis) and as Corporate Treasurer. Her particular love is classical astrology and how it can be applied today.